OPTIMIZATION

Unlock product growth by engaging long-tail users

Lizard Optimization
Unlock product growth by engaging long-tail users

PRINT ISBN: 978-0-9930881-7-9

Published 1 September 2024

Copyright © Gojko Adzic
Author: Gojko Adzic
Copy-editor: Mary White
Design and layout: Nikola Korac

Neuri Consulting LLP
Suite A, 1st Floor
62 Goldsworth Road
Woking, Surrey GU21 6LQ
United Kingdom
contact@neuri.com

CONTENTS

ACCIDENTAL FOREWORD

Daniel Terhorst-North,
technologist, business optimiser
and product enthusiast

There are many famous pivots in product history. Flickr started as a multiplayer game which had a facility for uploading game screenshots and chatting about them. Over time, the people at Flickr noticed that users were uploading photos of their cats or holidays and chatting about those instead. Eventually, the developers dropped the game altogether and built a successful photo uploading and sharing product.

In *Lizard Optimization*, Gojko Adzic explores what it would mean to turn this kind of happy accident into a deliberate product strategy. He is careful to qualify it as only one tool in the product manager's toolkit, but I am more bullish than this and can imagine it as a primary product growth strategy.

The English philosopher and theologian G.K. Chesterton proposed a thought experiment in which you find a fence built across a road. Of course, your first instinct would be to remove the fence; it is clearly dangerous! Chesterton warns that you should not attempt to remove the fence until you have found out why it was placed there in the first place. Only then can you determine whether it is safe to remove it.

Lizard Optimization looks at the same situation *as though you were a fence manufacturer*! "Why would someone put one of my fences there, across a road? That makes no sense!" The Chesterton student would be learning about empathy and the value of situational awareness and context. The fence manufacturer would be more curious about why someone isn't using its fence to keep cows in a field like everyone else.

This is the essence of Lizard Optimization: first, to notice that someone is using your product in a "weird" way; second to understand what they are really trying to do – in the language of the Jobs-to-be-Done theory, what job they want to do – and then to make it easier for them, with the indirect goal of making the product better for many more potential customers.

As Schopenhauer observed, "the problem is not so much to see what nobody has yet seen, as to think what nobody has yet thought about what everybody sees." Anyone can see people "misusing" a product and write them off as "non-technical" or worse. The lizard optimizer looks deeper than this. One person's strange behaviour is another person's product opportunity.

While reading this book, I have already experienced several situations where a lizard's-eye view would have created a better product, and I am now questioning how often a Lizard Optimization was hiding in plain sight. I will certainly be keeping my eye out for them from now on!

INTRODUCTION

A product I worked on grew explosively from November 2021 to November 2022. The key user metric, tracking when people are getting value from the product, increased by more than 500 times in those 12 months (times, not percent). This happened after a period of unremarkable growth and a slow decline. Looking back, the key factor in reversing the decline and unlocking exponential growth was a counter-intuitive approach to engaging users.

This book is a summary of what I learned from that crazy growth phase, synthesized into a simple process that you can apply to improve your products. As a consequence, this process can help you unlock growth, reduce churn and increase revenue.

Who should read this book?

This book is primarily for software product managers, product data scientists, senior engineers and anyone else involved in product management and guidance.

If your role involves coming up with new feature ideas, approving or rejecting proposed changes, or supporting people who do, this is a book for you. On the other hand, if you're reading this expecting to find competitive hairdressing tips for your bearded dragon, I'm afraid you've picked up the wrong Lizard Optimization book.

How can Lizard Optimization help you?

If your product is still looking for a market, Lizard Optimization can help you find it sooner. For products that need to grow their user base, this technique can help you reduce churn and keep customers engaged for longer. For more mature products, Lizard Optimization could uncover new feature ideas, engage overlooked categories of users, and help you address larger markets. It can also reveal interesting ideas for increasing customer lifetime value.

The basics of the process emerged during early development of MindMup, an online mind-mapping application, mostly as a way to make the product so good that word of mouth could replace marketing (a more cynical version would be to say that we didn't have money for ads). The process matured during development of Narakeet, a text-to-speech narration and video generator (which at some point had money for ads, but we were too stupid to make them work). Most of the stories in this book are from one of those two products. Others are anecdotes that might one day get me in trouble, but I've included anyway for your entertainment.

Treat this book as an early case study, shining light on something that could be interesting to try out. It's intended as a working manual. Feel free to highlight sections, scribble on these pages, or use the book to prop up a wobbly desk leg as required. (Although I'd advise against the latter if you're reading this book on a Kindle...)

Help to evolve the practice

The Lizard Optimization process isn't complete, and I expect it to evolve over the next few years with the involvement of the community. I'd like to include you in turning Lizard Optimization into something that can be helpful to a large part of our industry. Please get in touch with ideas, complaints, stories or even if you just want a sounding board for experiments. Let me know what you tried, what worked and what failed, and together we can come up with better ways to make successful products. My email is *gojko@neuri.com*. (And, just in case anything inspires you to give your bearded dragon a hipster haircut, photos of that are also welcome; thanks for sticking around.)

FROM DOOM TO BOOM

One of the products that inspired me to write about Lizard Optimization is Narakeet, a text-to-speech voiceover and video maker. The public beta-testing phase for Narakeet completed in October 2020, with people building more than 100,000 videos. Out of this we got a small core of super-engaged users who were enthusiastic and seemed to be getting a lot of value out of the product. After Narakeet switched to a commercial model in October 2020, the initial stats looked very promising. Slightly fewer than 10,000 users stayed on, and roughly 2% of those converted to a commercial plan. Although those numbers were quite small, the fact that people were using the product actively, and some were even willing to pay for the experience, was confirmation that it made sense to continue. The product soon became nicely profitable and I no longer had to sink my personal money into it. That was a big moment. I even treated myself to a new pot plant for my desk. Unfortunately, the plant lasted longer than most of our users.

A year later, things were looking dire. Activity fell to fewer than 100 new videos created each day. The web traffic kept declining for months. People who discovered the product through Google Search weren't trying it for long enough to become truly engaged. All the key metrics were dropping, despite months of attempts to reverse them. The product was still profitable – but barely, and it wouldn't stay that way for long. Unless a miracle happened quickly, Narakeet was on its way to a digital trash can (the plant was becoming concerned about its future as well).

I bootstrapped development (there was no external investment), so the budget for marketing was quite restricted. This meant that Narakeet would need to compete on quality, not on marketing. In *Product-Led Growth*, Wes Bush calls such types of growth "product-led", as opposed to "sales-led". With a product-led model, most new customers come as a result of inbound product usage rather than enterprise sales and outbound activities. A "self-serve flywheel" of user engagement creates growth. (Again, this mostly applies to software products. Please don't try making a self-serve flywheel if you're running a restaurant.)

Product-led growth worked amazingly well for MindMup, a product I co-founded in the early 2010s. Satisfied users and word of mouth were more than enough to turn MindMup into a moderate success, and I was hoping to repeat that with Narakeet. Unfortunately, the Software-as-a-Service space seemed to be a lot more saturated in the early 2020s than it had been 10 years earlier, there was a lot more competition, and none of the tricks that worked for MindMup were helping Narakeet to turn the tide.

During the first half of 2021 we hired two different groups of growth consultants to help with ideas for different strategies to try out, but nothing paid off. The first group delivered a PowerPoint with 70 slides of "key steps". The other provided very convincing guidance that was as effective as astrology. For example, advertising on Instagram was described as a "sure bet" by the second group of consultants, and led to exactly zero new customers.

I firmly decided not to pour any more personal money into the product, and projected that the financials would become unsustainable around the end of the year 2021. However, I didn't want to disappoint the remaining commercial users. My plan was to stop new registrations and just keep the product running for existing customers until their accounts ran out. Because the product uses a freemium model, and commercial users are effectively paying for free trials, stopping new registrations would make it financially sustainable but kill all future growth options.

As preparation for putting the product on ice, I started to look for ways to reduce support costs and make everything run on its own. I tried to identify the crazy stuff that was making the product explode, or complex parts of the user interface which caused users to get into trouble. The goal was to polish all those sharp edges so that the product could run without anyone having to read and respond to customer emails every day.

After two months working only on outliers, edge cases and weird accidents, the miracle we were waiting for actually started to happen. Instead of just preventing the current group of users from hitting a dead end, the changes to the product caused users to become more engaged. A lot more. They started to create more videos. But this wasn't just the obvious case of a more polished product leading to more usage. Optimizing the product for one of the weird outliers unlocked a completely new market. A small percentage of people wanted to create audio files instead of videos. Helping them succeed was either a stroke of genius or a stroke of luck, I still can't decide. New users started to create a lot more audio files than videos. Several orders of magnitude more.

With amazing serendipity, we also found a consultant for online marketing whose thinking and method were focused on the product itself, not on the alignment of stars with the zodiac. He helped reverse the search traffic trends. Google was sending us more people, who were getting better engaged and bringing more new users as a result. With a combination of a better product and better content, the "self-serve flywheel" started to turn.

When, previously, product usage had been dropping uncontrollably, we had tried to focus on the largest set of users where our work could deliver the biggest impact. This seemed like common sense. This approach led to a slow death for the product. Once we started to focus on the outliers, things took a turn for the better. Instead of running out of money by end of 2021, as predicted, Narakeet started to grow exponentially.

We changed tactics and started to systematically look for outliers and optimize the product for them. This also helped me see in a new light some hugely successful things we'd done for MindMup and Narakeet, which I'd previously considered happy accidents. A product optimization process started to crystallize from that.

For the next 12 months, we applied this kind of optimization a dozen times with Narakeet. Active usage increased from 150-200 audio/video tasks per day to roughly 100,000 daily file conversions. This corresponds to about 500 times year-on-year growth.

The best part of that experience is that the growth didn't come as a result of bombarding users with ads, annoying them with sales calls or forcing people to sign unfavourable contracts. It was a direct consequence of helping users succeed and creating a genuinely better product. The optimization process that evolved throughout that period is what I now call Lizard Optimization, and the topic of this book. (Why lizards? I'll explain that in the next chapter.)

Turn inexplicable to invaluable

Unlocking exponential growth from an outlier edge case isn't that uncommon, but today it mostly happens as a lucky accident, often after a lot of opposition from the product management team, who want to keep the focus on the primary users.

There's a lovely example of that in the book *Founders at Work* by Jessica Livingston. In the late nineties, some super-smart people figured out how to efficiently compute cryptographic algorithms on low-powered

devices, and they built a company around an idea to transfer digital cash over PalmPilot mobile computers. (For readers who were born after the dot-com boom and don't know what a PalmPilot was, imagine something that looks like a hybrid of a smartphone and a dumb phone, with Internet access but without an actual phone. I would say "it looked a bit like a Game Boy", but then I'd have to explain what one of those was too!)

To promote the PalmPilot application on the emerging World Wide Web, the company also launched a simple but functional demo web site. The expectation was that people could try the key features easily using the web site and then download the PalmPilot app to use it frequently. "The web site was unsexy and we didn't really care", said one of those super-smart cryptographers in an interview for Livingston's book.

The PalmPilot app didn't really catch on. Web site traffic, on the other hand, was booming. This was "inexplicable" because "the handheld device was cool and the web site was just a demo". The audience was using the web site to transfer money for online auctions.

The company was "fighting, tooth and nail, crazy eBay people", telling them they weren't wanted. But the "crazy" people didn't care. They kept using the web site and not the "cool" PalmPilot app.

By the end of the year 2000, the web site had 1.5 million users. The PalmPilot app peaked at about 12,000 users. The company killed the handheld device app and focused on web-based money transfer. Today, it's one of the biggest online payment processors in the world, and you probably know it as PayPal.

Turn exceptions to extensions

This book is my attempt to make the process of product discovery from unusual usage patterns systematic, instead of just relying on happy accidents. By treating it as an explicit process, I hope that people will start accepting discovery based on outliers as something normal rather than an exception, and skip the phase where product management fight against it. Instead, we can use that time to make our products genuinely better and facilitate growth.

LEARN THE LIZARD LOGIC

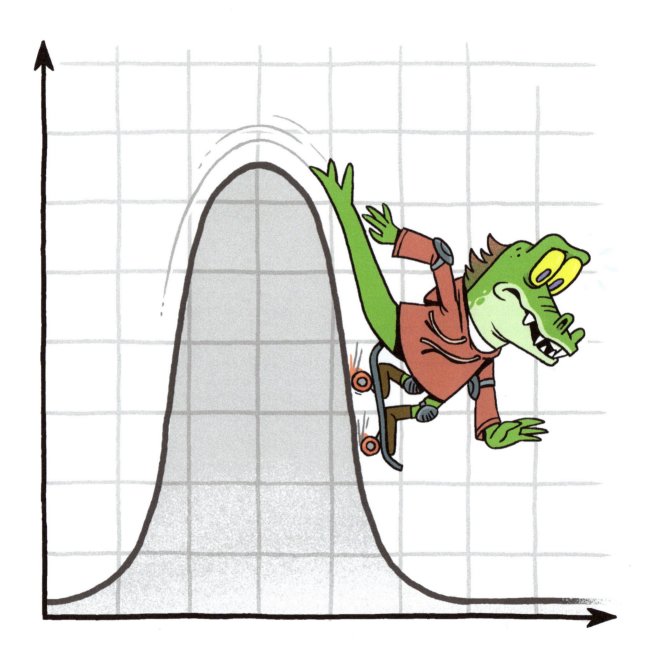

In statistical jargon, the "long tail" is the part of the distribution curve far from the central part. The long tail contains infrequent, unusual and abnormal data points. This is where the outliers live. Looking at what our users do with our products, the events in the long tail often don't seem to have been caused by rational humans.

Scott Alexander of the *Slate Star Codex* blog tackled the problem of understanding long-tail outliers in an article titled *Beware of Phantom Lizardmen*. Reviewing a study combining demographic data with a psychological test, Alexander noted that one person listed "male" as their nationality and "American" as their gender. An honest mistake, perhaps. However, several people listed "Martian" as their nationality. (If you're reading in 2050, just bear in mind that I wrote this before the founding of the Martian Congressional Republic.)

At first sight, it's easy to dismiss these choices as crazy. Dig a bit deeper and you'll find plenty of reasons why someone reasonable could do something we perceive as dumb. They could be distracted, confused or disinterested. Some people don't care enough to do the correct thing, even if they know how. Some people just do the wrong thing out of spite.

Each of these individual cases might be an infrequent outlier, but when the people affected by all those factors are combined, they become a significant group. Quoting US Public Policy Polling research from 2013 about conspiracy theories (which included beliefs that lizardmen secretly rule the world), Scott Alexander suggests that as much as 4% of the research population are doing inexplicable things. He calls it the "Lizardman's Constant".

Although the Lizardman's Constant is a joke rule, I find it quite interesting to consider the lizardmen when dealing with crazy outlier events in my work. As a product starts to get popular, some percentage of the users will do crazy things. At first these actions might seem beyond any normal reason, as if driven by lizard logic and not human brains. Scratch the surface a bit and things may not seem so crazy any more.

Sometimes you'll find people who select the wrong option because they're temporarily distracted. The user interface might be confusing for some users, causing them to click the wrong button. Some percentage of your users will be visually impaired, colourblind or try to use your product under direct sunlight on a beach. Some will have thicker than usual thumbs or not have enough dexterity in their fingers to accurately choose between two small buttons placed close together. Some people will be curious and press all the buttons to see what happens. And of course, some will be what Dungeons & Dragons players call "chaotic evil"; they will mess with you simply because they enjoy breaking things.

Inspired by Alexander's article, I started calling the outliers lizards. The name reminds everyone that we're dealing with events from the long tail of the statistical distribution. It also provides much-needed comic relief when faced with a brain-melting puzzle. Hence the name Lizard Optimization.

Finding the lizards is a great starting point for improvements. To do crazy things with your product, lizard users have to already know about it, expect some value, and decide that it's worth their time to engage with you. The marketing and acquisition work for those users is already done. However, something is preventing them from succeeding in their goals. Understanding this lizard behaviour is crucial to discovering true user problems.

Lizardman's Constant is 4%

Listen to your lizards

A few years ago we had a curious case of an educator who wanted to block his students from using certain functions in MindMup. The professor asked us how to lock down the user interface. This request went directly against our vision to create an easy and flexible way to map out ideas. However, educational institutions are one of our key markets, so we engaged with the user to try to understand his real needs instead of simply dismissing the request.

MindMup had become popular in schools, and we often simplified the user interface for children. The person contacting us, however, was a university professor, and his users were undergraduate philosophy students, not kids with a limited understanding of technology. This meant that user-interface complexity wasn't an issue.

Instead, the professor was using a specific type of visualization to show the logic of reasoning in philosophical arguments. That type of visualization had rigid rules around shapes and colours. From one perspective, this had nothing to do with the primary use of our product. From a different perspective, this was potentially a new way for us to expand in the educational market.

Instead of allowing administrators to block application functions, we implemented a set of templates and shortcuts to manage argument visualizations easily, and this became hugely influential. Several major universities started to use MindMup as a result.

Don't dismiss long-tail outliers. You may not want to address all of the freak cases, but understanding them is invaluable to make the product genuinely good. That's what Lizard Optimization is about. Helping lizards succeed forces us to make our products more accessible and usable, improving the user experience for everyone. This can significantly improve user retention. Discovering people who have unexpected needs often points to new usage types and potentially improving the product to serve wider audiences. This can significantly increase new user acquisition. These two factors – existing user retention and new user acquisition – are the key levers influencing product growth.

Once you have some attention, double down on retention

When we pare down product growth to the very basics, only two numbers influence it. (To keep things simple for now, let's ignore your daily caffeine intake.) The first measures how many new people join. The second measures how many people leave. Lots of smart books apply different terminology to these two numbers, divide the user-engagement funnel into parts, and split people into categories such as leads, users, customers and so on, but the fundamentals remain. Add the people joining, subtract the people leaving, and if the difference is positive the product usage grows. If the difference is negative then the product is in trouble. (That's probably when you should increase the caffeine).

The tug of war between acquisition and retention gives us two ways to speed up growth: one is to find more users; the other is to keep them engaged for longer. Naively speaking, influencing either by the same amount should produce the same result, but this ignores an important timing component. Improving retention boosts the effects of any future acquisition, so it can have compound effects.

During the very early stages of the product development, we can only focus on acquiring new users. After all, there's not much point figuring out how to keep

people around if no people are there to start with. However, the balance shifts very quickly, and user retention becomes critically important. In fact, the most successful companies don't even try to aggressively pursue growth until they achieve great retention numbers. In *Lean Analytics*, Alistair Croll and Benjamin Yoskovitz argue that optimizing "stickiness" before growth is critical for success.

Making a product "sticky" is also critical for profitability. Amy Gallo, in the article *The Value of Keeping the Right Customers* published in the October 2014 issue of the *Harvard Business Review*, suggests that increasing customer retention is a disproportionally powerful lever for profit. Based on research by Frederick Reichheld, Gallo claims that improving retention by 5% can increase profit anywhere from 25% to 95%. Of course, this doesn't mean we can ignore acquisition. After all, we can only retain the users that we've acquired. However, improving retention can have disproportionally effective results, and it might be much easier to influence than acquisition.

Attracting new customers mostly relies on external factors. It involves marketing, buying ads, or relying on others to spread word of mouth. In contrast, customer retention is something that a product can do on its own. If your responsibility is to influence product design or development, as I assume most people reading this book will be doing, then you can impact retention a lot more than you can impact acquisition.

Unless you've skipped or completely fumbled initial research (oh, hey Quibi, didn't see you there!), the majority of your users won't help you figure out how to improve retention, at least not significantly. The product is already designed to help them. You need to look for inspiration in the blind spots and help long-tail users succeed. You need to optimize the product for lizards!

Once you've got people's attention, put extra effort into their retention.

OPTIMIZING FOR LIZARDS

Lizard Optimization is a technique for designing product development experiments by engaging long-tail users that seem to follow some unexplainable "lizard" logic. It can help you understand your audience better and improve your products. I've used the method to significantly enhance existing user interactions, develop new features and even discover a completely new direction for a product, opening up an untapped market.

There are four key steps to Lizard Optimization. You can remember them by their starting letters, **LZRD**:

1. **L**earn how people are misusing your product
2. **Z**ero in on one behaviour change
3. **R**emove obstacles to user success
4. **D**etect unintended impacts

There's also a less formal and shorter variant that's easier to remember:

5. **L**izard Alert
6. **Z**oom
7. **R**escue
8. **D**ouble-check

This chapter is a short introduction to the whole process, so you can use it as a quick reference. The chapters that follow explain each of these steps in detail.

Step 1: Learn how people are misusing your product

With an infinite amount of time and money for research, it would be easy to predict all the ways in which people might interact with our products. Without that, we're left with imperfect insight. Even the best product managers will guess some things wrong. To do the right things, we need to balance upfront research and design with cheaper alternatives. These include two very powerful tools for product management: surprise and feedback.

To let feedback do its magic, product managers must first allow themselves to be surprised. We need to look beyond just confirming our assumptions, especially in situations where the stakeholders are so overconfident that they feel their product deserves the next Millennium Technology Prize. This means investigating the unexpected and the unknown.

In particular, feedback about unintended usage paths is crucial unlock growth. If you want to grow your product audience, you should constantly be on the lookout for user workarounds and hacks. Do you know how people are misusing, abusing or tweaking your products? Unintended usage paths can point to incomplete or problematic features, but they can also lead you to previously undiscovered user goals and untapped market opportunities.

One reason why Lizard Optimization has so much power is that we can tap into the vast quantity of information about existing users that's already available but currently unused. If a customer is willing to use a product in a suboptimal way, then we can assume that the specific usage pattern solves an actual problem for that person. It might be a twist on the problem that we assumed our customers have. Or, it might not even be the same problem that we originally intended to solve. We can use that information to understand our users and customers in depth and find their real problems.

The first step in Lizard Optimization is to find the people who do unusual, unexpected and unexplainable things with your product. For example, someone trying to eat pizza from a coffee cup.

Step 2: Zero in on one behaviour change

The long tail of the distribution curve, by definition, stretches a very long way. When we start looking for the unexpected, unplanned and unusual, some things we encounter will start to resemble a freak show. Some will be nuggets of amazing insight. Some will just be irrelevant garbage. But there will be no shortage of potential ideas.

With a time-to-market deadline in our lifetimes, it won't be possible to act on all of the feedback. And even if we could magically perform everything, it doesn't mean we should. (Yes, your mobile app may be tricky to navigate for users wearing scuba flippers on their hands as part of an elaborate Halloween costume, but that's not necessarily an issue.) Ideally, we want to improve the product in ways that will help the large majority of users as well as the long tail. We also want our improvements to be consistent with current organizational and product objectives.

In order to focus our efforts and deliver the largest impact, we need to select one area to improve. If the first step is figuring out the source of the noise in our product usage analytics, then the second step is about finding the signal in that noise. We can go deeper into one behaviour and understand why it happens, trying to decipher the lizard logic.

Step 3: Remove obstacles to user success

The third step in Lizard Optimization is to help our users become more successful at interacting with the product. The previous step helped us focus on one specific behaviour change and consolidate long-tail feedback into improvement ideas. We can now look for patterns, investigate user workflows, and figure out potential bottlenecks and obstacles to user success. We can then think of ideas that may help users succeed better, faster, more easily or more frequently. (A good soundtrack for step 3 would be Daft Punk's "Harder, Better, Faster, Stronger".)

In the third step, we take action based on the insights from the first two steps. We design and track engagement funnels, trying out the improvement ideas as reversible experiments until we can spot positive change in our long-tail user behaviour.

Step 4: Detect unintended impacts

Lizards, by definition, have their own logic. They behave in unexpected and unpredictable ways. Sometimes, our actions might have a completely opposite effect from the one we intended. Also, tweaking a product to help one group of users might have unexpected effects for another group. Different user groups have different needs, and the needs sometimes even conflict with each other. (Hard to imagine when we spend our time in the 100% conflict-free world of product managers, engineers and sales teams, I know...)

To prevent partial solutions or negative effects, it's important to closely monitor for unintended impacts. Surprise is a wonderful tool, but to get the benefits from it, we need to put ourselves in a situation where we can be surprised. We can then use this feedback to improve future experiments.

When can you use Lizard Optimization?

The ideas in this book should be applicable to products where you want to grow market share, reduce churn or increase revenue. There are three important prerequisites: at least some active usage, iterative development, and the need for growth.

Lizard Optimization relies on analysing what people are actually doing with your product, as opposed to what you expected them to do. In order to analyse that information, there must be some folks to look at. If your product has no active users, then it's too early to apply Lizard Optimization. There are lots of good customer or user-experience research techniques that you can try first.

If the product is very mature and you don't need to grow it any more, then Lizard Optimization is pointless. It's much better to focus on consolidation, technical scaling and reducing operating costs.

If you just want to increase the audience or sales without changing any product features or releasing a new version, then Lizard Optimization can't help.

What are the limitations?

Lizard Optimization isn't a growth hack. It won't help you get rich quick or magically reverse hair loss. (In fact, struggling to understand lizards will likely make you pull some hair out.) It's a systematic way to figure out your user-engagement blind spots and address them, so you can make genuinely better products.

This process isn't a full development methodology and doesn't solve all the potential challenges of modern product delivery. It's just one tool you should have in your product management arsenal. If you feel stuck, try Lizard Optimization for a bit. Once you unlock growth, follow that path for a while using other techniques. Come back to Lizard Optimization later when you feel stuck again.

LEARN HOW PEOPLE ARE MISUSING YOUR PRODUCT

A good product manager needs to balance addressing two big risks. On one side, there's the danger of delivering the wrong thing. On the other side, there's the risk of shipping too late. Lots of research methods evolved to reduce the first risk, but they're effectively constrained by the second one. Time is valuable, especially time to market, so research needs to stop at some point to make way for actual product development and delivery. Because of that, even the best researchers might not spot some things upfront. This is why it's critically important to look for feedback after the actual product is in the hands of users.

Feedback can prove that people are doing what we expect, which is important to show that the product is going in the right direction; but it can open the doors to much more. If we use feedback after launch to discover the unexpected, not just to confirm the expected, then delivery can complement research and help to unlock product market growth.

Lizard optimizers actively seek to learn how people are misusing, abusing or tweaking their products. Discovering that someone is misusing a product is wonderful, because it means that actual people are investing additional effort and time in interacting with the results of our work. Users wouldn't be doing that unless those interactions were providing something valuable, which is a great confirmation that the product is actually useful. People might be getting value in a way that we didn't expect, or getting a different type of value, but it's value nevertheless. (Even if seeing how they're misunderstanding your beautiful creation does initially make you want to hurl.) And that's a great starting point for further development.

Looking for unintended product usage addresses more than just the gaps in the initial research. It helps us spot changes in the user behaviour caused by our products. That kind of insight can't come from research before delivery, because the actual product is causing the change. Bruce Tognazzini formulated this as the *Complexity Paradox*: "[when] we reduce the complexity people experience in a given task, people will take on a more challenging task". Once the first version of a product is released, users will apply it to solve some problem and then use the time they saved to attack a different problem. Or they'll find ways to apply the product to new, bigger problems which we may not have planned for.

Discovering that people are using our products in unexpected ways can help us learn about the more challenging tasks or bigger problems that our users are experiencing. Feedback on the unexpected can uncover new user goals or use cases that we might've overlooked in research. It can also point to related jobs that users need to perform, showing potential directions in which the product needs to evolve. A great example of that is the total surprise we encountered when adding content security policies to Narakeet…

By Hanlon's beard, why is Google hacking my users?

Hackers and browser developers are playing an arms race, with one side finding ever more ingenious ways of tricking users into revealing sensitive data, and the other trying to prevent gullible people from hurting themselves. (Which reminds me: Grandma, if you're reading this, I will never email asking you to transfer money. Not when Grandpa's such a soft target.) That's why modern browsers block lots of old web technologies.

One legacy web feature that's not so easy to drop is the embedding of third-party content, where one web site includes images or data from another site. There are still lots of genuine use cases for sharing content across web sites, but this approach is also used by scammers to impersonate banking web pages and trick victims into revealing log-in information. A web standard called the Content Security Policy emerged in recent years to help web sites restrict sharing and protect themselves from malicious reuse.

We introduced content security policies relatively early into Narakeet, but not from the start. Once restrictions were in place, we could see whether anyone was trying to scam our users. To my big surprise, hundreds of users per day loaded our content from some third-party web site, which seemed like an outright scam. I was surprised that hackers were already targeting our product, as it was still very small. There wasn't much to steal, unless the thief was *really* into PowerPoint presentations.

All the blocked requests came from a web site that started with "narakeet" and ended with a curious domain, ".goog". This wasn't one of our domains, yet genuine users were accessing our content through that web site, potentially having their credentials stolen. Digging deeper into the .goog web sites that were potentially spying on our users, I traced them back to Google. Why on earth was Google trying to hack our users?

Hanlon's razor, a humorous rule from *Murphy's Law Book Two* by Arthur Bloch, states that we should "never attribute to malice that which is adequately explained by stupidity". Rather than raising a red alert, I started to consider that we were actually dealing with lizards. Hundreds of our users were willingly allowing Google to intercept communication between us and them. But why?

Hanlon's razor might be a joke, but there's a serious version of it in *The Failure of Risk Management* by Douglas Hubbard: "Never attribute to malice or stupidity that which can be explained by moderately rational individuals following incentives in a complex system." Translated to plain English, this means that we should first figure out what the crazies are doing, then figure out their incentives, and all of a sudden those people might not look so crazy any more. What incentives could my "moderately rational" lizards have in this complex system of interactions for allowing Google to spy on them? Well, for a start, wanting to use the product without speaking the language of the user interface. The web site content was in English. Some of the users couldn't read English, but they still enthusiastically wanted to use our product. They resorted to using Google's translation engine. Go to the Google Translate web site but, instead of a sentence, paste a URL into the source language box. Google Translate will show a web link in the destination language box. Click it, and your browser will open a new window, showing the translated web site content. To work around the security limitations of modern browsers, Google Translate automatically creates a web site on the .goog domain and uses it to intercept all user communication between the user and the original web site. Noble or insidious, that's difficult to say, but it was happening nevertheless.

I can understand why someone would want to translate a web page with interesting content to read, but trying to translate an application automatically sounds crazy. As a developer, I'm not sure how someone could even think that would work. But people obviously did. From my perspective, this was an obvious case of lizard logic. From the users' perspective, they probably expected everything to just work out of the box. People were trying to use a translated web site, and it was broken. We were losing potential customers.

We absolutely do not want to allow users to expose their sensitive data to third parties, but they should at

least have a good first experience with the web site and understand what's going on. We rewrote some parts of the application flow to expect working in an automatically translated context, and presented users with a reasonable error message to help them understand why their content is blocked and how to fix it. A meaningful error message isn't really a solution, but it can be a good starting point. (Besides, sometimes it's just cathartic to tell people "What you're doing is wrong!")

The next step was to implement deeper support for automated translation in the browser. In addition to Google Translate's horrible method which enables spying on users, modern browsers also offer inline translation without creating a cloned web site and exposing sensitive information. Making that work properly became an important task, and it only required minor changes to the web site to mark up certain things that

shouldn't be translated at all. As a result of inline translation working nicely, our users created lots of YouTube videos showing how to use the application with automated (in-browser) translation, helping people in their communities benefit from our application and bringing us new users from untapped markets.

Against the advice of the marketing consultants, we introduced content in other languages. At the time when I wrote this, the three most popular pages on the web site by Google Search activity were in Spanish, Hindi and Russian. (Sorry, marketing consultants! Or should I say, "¡Lo siento!") Huge amounts of traffic, users and revenue come from people who don't speak English. I completely missed this insight in early user research, because I only interviewed people who spoke English. This was both a limitation of the need to speak a common language during the interviews, and a conscious (but ultimately wrong) decision to focus first on the English-speaking market. Internationalization was always in the plan, but for much, much later. Spotting that our application was becoming popular with people who didn't speak English changed the development priorities quite a bit.

Feedback about unexpected behaviours was crucial to discover this insight. To learn about similar issues, we can't rely on what people say. We need to observe what they actually do.

Get the outer view, not the interview

If you ever feel that you could use a touch more masochism in your life, go and watch someone try to use your product in a user-experience test. I still remember the pain of the first serious UX test for MindMup, even though it was more than 10 years ago at the time when I wrote this. There are some wounds, it seems, that no amount of therapy can heal.

MindMup started with the idea of enabling people to quickly brainstorm and capture ideas using mind maps online. Web applications and cloud storage were slowly becoming acceptable to mainstream users, so we jumped on the opportunity to create a cloud-based tool that was as fast as a desktop application but not constrained by the limitations of working on a single computer.

Our initial usability target was that a new user, someone who's never seen our tool before, would be able to create and share a simple mind map in less than five minutes. This target provided a wonderful constraint which forced us to make the user interface very simple. The initial version had a floating toolbar with about a dozen tools represented by intuitive icons, and a top menu with just three buttons. The primary action button, in the top right, allowed users to save their map to

our cloud storage. The other two buttons, in the top-left corner, allowed users to create a new map and to access previously saved maps. The button for saving the content was obviously labelled "Save", but putting a label on the other two buttons was a bit more tricky. We settled on "Create a new map" and "My maps". This all seemed very intuitive, obvious and easy to use.

We did a bunch of interviews for the initial product design, but putting the product in front of people and observing from the outside uncovered a ton of blind spots from our research. Jakob Nielsen says that "don't listen to users" is the first rule of usability. (Of course, "don't listen to project managers" is the zeroth rule.) Nielsen suggests that watching what people actually do is significantly more relevant for design feedback than what people say they do, or want to do in the future.

Almost everyone in the first test spent two or three minutes just trying to figure out how to create a blank map. That's half the time we allowed for the full process, and they couldn't even get started. As I observed people move the mouse cursor over a button with a big bold label "Create a new map" and not click it, my stomach began to turn. Everyone was looking for the "File" menu with an item called "New". It didn't matter that people were creating maps, not files, and that the maps lived in the cloud and not on people's local devices. Users expected the File menu, and the application didn't have it.

In an effort to remove unnecessary clutter, we had oversimplified the user interface to the point where it wasn't intuitive any more. It's as if we had found a way to make a door open without a handle, but people were so used to interacting with hundreds of doors with the same old handles that they'd learned to expect them and couldn't use our sci-fi door. In effect, we had made a "Norman door".

In *The Design of Everyday Things*, Don Norman shows lots of examples of seemingly clever design that just confuses people because they intuitively expect something else. Our product was clever in the wrong places.

The audience was used to desktop applications, and we hadn't considered how important that was. A small number of our trial users were even trying to access a context menu by clicking the right mouse button. MindMup is a web application, running inside a browser, so the right-click showed the standard browser context menu. Some of our users were so immersed that they seemed to forget that they were interacting with a web site. Users would notice the toolbar quickly after the right-click, so this wasn't a major issue, but it still bothered me.

Replacing the top-bar options with a standard File menu was a no-brainer; the UX tests clearly showed that we should do that. Changing the right-click menu

was a much more difficult decision. On one hand, only a few users experienced the issue with the right-click menu – not enough to make general conclusions. They all found alternative ways of interacting with the application (thankfully very few of which involved four-letter words), so the missing menu wasn't a critical issue. On the other hand, we wanted to keep users productive, and it felt bad to break the immersion. But then again, some expected the standard browser menu when they clicked on the right mouse button (I definitely did). Any change to the context menu would perhaps have unintended effects for other people. After a bit of discussion that led nowhere, we decided to run a reversible experiment and change the right-click menu for a few weeks to see whether anyone complained.

It turns out that we changed the right-click menu at a fantastically opportune time. A week after we added the context menu controls, MindMup was reviewed on Lifehacker, then one of the most popular productivity web sites globally. The reviewer praised our productivity tweaks, in particular the right-click button menu. This review was syndicated to other Lifehacker sites and was also widely pirated and translated into other languages. Lots of other productivity bloggers wrote about MindMup. A month later, thousands of new pages had linked to our product web site, significantly helping with search engine rankings. We started appearing within the first five positions for many key phrases on Google Search. This resulted in years of high-volume traffic and a lot of recurring revenue. Not bad at all for a tool that had effectively launched just a few months before.

If I'd tried to guess the value of the right-click menu change upfront, I'd have missed by a wide margin. I thought it was a minor tweak that might help some fringe users be a bit more productive. But it turned out to be one of the most important things we ever did. And we'd never have thought about it on our own. Instead, this was a direct result of us going out to users and looking for unforeseen ways in which they interacted with our product. We were actively seeking to understand our blind spots and what was hiding behind them. That was painful and costly, but it was several orders of magnitude cheaper than paying for advertising to get the equivalent traffic as the top spots on Google.

Scale the UX test cringe

The UX testing cringe is a wonderful feedback mechanism. When your stomach hurts as you observe someone struggling with your product, the experience sticks and forces you to make better product management decisions (and/or reevaluate your relationship with gluten). Yet, this process is expensive and doesn't scale well. It's not exactly easy to sit behind tens of thousands of users and observe them in action. But we

need to do exactly that to manage Lizard Optimization repeatedly and at scale.

Many good techniques for user research with large populations rely on interviews or questionnaires. They're valuable tools, but not for Lizard Optimization. Interviews and questionnaires are great for situations when you roughly know what you want to learn, particularly if you want to select between several predefined product directions. They're good for what the former US defence secretary Donald Rumsfeld in 2002 called "known unknowns".

Lizard Optimization starts in the category of questions Rumsfeld called "unknown unknowns", suggesting that "it is the latter category that tends to be the difficult ones". It's very difficult to ask good questions about things hidden behind our blind spots. The first step of Lizard Optimization is to get operational awareness about those unplanned user interactions. Don't limit feedback to just confirmation that people do the expected. Try to shine a light on your blind spots as well.

Here are four good ways of observing users at scale and detecting unexpected actions:

- Record and investigate user workflow errors
- Find out how people are "hacking" your product
- Track support patterns
- Engage with outliers personally

Record and investigate user workflow errors

Narakeet allows people to read aloud the content from many types of files, such as Word, Excel and PDF documents. A few users every day try to upload something the product doesn't yet support. Like most applications, Narakeet shows the user a nice error message, helping them understand why the action doesn't work. In addition to that, the product sends information about such user errors back to us for analysis (and, occasionally, a good laugh). This is a gold-mine for product ideas.

For example, some people upload photographs of handwritten notes. I can kind of see the logic in expecting software to read them, but accurate hand-writing recognition is beyond the scope of what we can do (especially as most look like scribbles on the back of a McDonald's

wrapper). A few people every day try to upload an APK file (Android application package). It's very difficult to see the logic in that. My best guess is that it's a modern version of dropping a malicious USB stick outside an office building and hoping that someone will load it. Some people try to load audio or video files, which is most likely a fat-finger error. (Though there's always the possibility it's a misguided singer-songwriter, doing whatever they can to get their music out there.)

Occasionally the workflow error analysis helps us spot an unintended use case that the product should support. (Not the music thing. I listened, and found it painfully derivative.) For example, a few people try to upload subtitle files every day. Subtitle files contain instructions for a video player to show a textual representation of an audio track, along with timestamps for when to show or hide that text. Someone uploading a subtitle file to a text-to-speech converter was unexpected but quite logical. People were trying to produce audio tracks to dub existing videos in a different language.

Dubbing videos in a different language is a usually a tedious, error-prone and time-consuming job, involving recording hundreds of small audio files and aligning them with the existing video. Because subtitle files already contained timestamps, we could speed up or slow down the voiceover to fit into the expected time and automatically align sound with the picture. The addition of subtitle conversion to Narakeet saved hours of work for people trying to produce alternative audio tracks. (Nice for them.) It's also one of the most profitable features of the product. (Nice for me.) Looking at the overall user population, only a tiny percentage need subtitle conversion. However, if you work in a corporate educational department and need to translate hundreds or thousands of videos, it's a godsend. And people in big corporate educational departments have big budgets to spend. As a result of having

you need a coffee top-up? Because break's over; you've got work to do…

If you do not have operational awareness of user mistakes, it's time to start tracking that kind of information. As a minimum, I suggest capturing basic contextual data whenever a user is shown any kind of error. You can then expand to collect details for a specific type of event when you're actively investigating it.

Tracking information about unintended user behaviour at scale can be quite a challenge, especially when you're trying to identify a signal in all the noise (and there will be more noise than at a Norwegian death-metal festival). Classic analytics tools that product managers are comfortable with, such as Google Analytics, are usually not good for this purpose. Such tools focus on visualizing the expected rather than the unexpected.

If you want to start tracking unintended user behaviour, check whether your organization is already using tools to capture application crashes or exceptions. Those tools tend to be better suited for this purpose. Over the last decade or so, the push to decentralize applications led to a need to monitor the different bits and pieces, in particular to identify technical issues. Tools that capture and analyse this information depend on the operating platforms for software, and there are too many variations of that to provide any kind of solid recommendation in a book. The tools are easy to find, though; just look for "real user monitoring", "exception tracking" or "crash analytics" tools or, slightly broader, search for "observability" or "telemetry" (not to be confused with "telepathy", although that would certainly help us understand the lizards). Most of these solutions are focused on capturing technical exceptions, but they're easy to tweak for sending custom events, such as when a user does something unexpected.

subtitle conversion we landed several huge customers, including some of the biggest spenders to date. This product development insight came directly as a result of tracking unexpected user uploads.

Take a break from reading this book now and think about your product. What happens when a user does something unexpected? Do you even know about it? Do you have the tools to track such exceptions within a large population of users? Can you tell whether it's one person doing something crazy or an emerging pattern of some new usage type? And most importantly, do

For web-based products, there's another class of tools that can be useful when trying to understand user errors. Session recorders can track everything that happens when a visitor browses your web site. You can then replay a particular session, kind of like watching a movie. Session-recording software can help you replicate the UX research experience of observing users in action, at scale. Watching all individual user sessions when you have even thousands of visitors isn't viable, but session recorders allow you to turn on recording selectively or search through sessions for specific events. A common trick to reduce the amount of information you need to look at is to start recording when users experience an error or do something unexpected. Most people will try again in case of an error; some may even try to solve the problem themselves or work around it. You can capture these actions for later inspection.

Collecting telemetry sometimes raises privacy and confidentiality concerns. You may need to balance the needs of product managers to collect accurate contextual information with the needs of users or enterprise customers to restrict data leaks. This is also why it's good to design custom reporting events for existing telemetry tools. Some common workarounds are to anonymize telemetry information and offer users an option to send feedback when they do something unexpected, instead of automatically phoning home. For example, early on for MindMup we tracked internally all the menu clicks performed by a user. This information was stored locally in the current user session, and not shared with us automatically. In case of an error, a user could submit feedback and we'd

For some up-to-date tool recommendations, check out lizardoptimization.org

also package the last 1000 menu clicks. This helped immensely to identify the paths users took to end up somewhere unintended, and it was a good tradeoff between seeing the complete picture and avoiding unnecessary behavioural tracking. (As a rule of thumb, you shouldn't be able to tell what a user is having for dinner tonight, unless you sold it to them.)

Find out how people are hacking your product

Other good places to look for unexpected insights are external sources, such as social media, forums and Q&A web sites. Check out what people are publishing about your products and try to identify unexpected or unpredicted usage types. Some people pride themselves on doing something cool and unexpected, and they like to boast when they make something useful. If a crazy use case brings your customers value, it might point to a new usage pattern or an area of growth.

At the start of 2023, the organic search traffic for Narakeet was picking up nicely. During January, Narakeet recorded about 500,000 search clicks from Google. With the increased web traffic, user engagement was growing as well, and in mid February people were producing about 100,000 audio and video files per day. Then we got an unexpected Valentine's day gift.

User engagement doubled on the 14th of February. Perhaps our loved-up users had introduced their dates to Narakeet by candlelight? Then it more than doubled again the next day. By the 16th of February, people were converting more than 500,000 files per day. On the 18th of February we got a congratulation email from Google, saying our site had passed 1 million search clicks in 28 days. This sounded like a justification to pop open some champagne, until I looked at the financials.

The people who came in the few days between the 14th and 18th of February mostly used up their free trial capacity but weren't converting to become commercial customers. Compared with the regular audience we were getting, people were dropping off from the funnel at a much higher rate. The audience was clearly getting enough benefit to engage until the end of the free trial, but not so much as to pay anything. Operational costs surged five times in a few days, revenue stayed the same, and the business was on a quick trajectory to bankruptcy.

Getting a sudden surge of interest is flattering, but this new traffic had to be blocked otherwise it would kill us. The majority of new Google search traffic was coming from India. As an emergency measure, we just blocked all free usage from India. That helped to reduce the flood but it didn't solve the problem fully. The traffic just shifted to other countries.

A few days earlier someone had published a YouTube video in Hindi on how to abuse our free tier and get unlimited audio conversions for free. I don't speak Hindi, but I played the video and noticed that they were using a VPN. (A VPN is a network tunnel that masks the outgoing Internet address.) This was tricking our detection of duplicated free accounts. VPN systems generally have connection points in many different countries, so when we blocked Indian traffic, abusers just started selecting other places to appear from.

Our Internet host has a relatively good way of detecting traffic coming from data centres instead of access providers. If traffic was coming from something like a data centre, that would usually mean that it originated from a bot or VPN tunnel. I couldn't think of any genuine reason why a person would access our site from a data centre, so we just blocked that. Instead of preventing a fifth of the world's population from becoming

our customers, we could just block people trying to hide from us. This wasn't a fool-proof way to stop VPN-tunnelling traffic, but it was quick and cheap. The free-tier abuse stopped almost immediately, operational costs went back to normal levels, and I quite enjoyed reading the negative comments on the YouTube video about how the trick no longer worked. On the other hand, I didn't enjoy receiving the hundreds of emails that followed.

Based on the drop in activity, it looked as if thousands of people had figured out the workaround on their own in previous months but were smart enough not to boast about it on YouTube. Once VPN access no longer worked, these people came out of the woodwork. Among the crazy complaints, one that stood out was from someone claiming that they needed to use a VPN because they were too spiritual for a regular Internet connection. Someone from an insurance company insisted that we turn their access back on, since it was critical for their business. According to the email, they'd been using Narakeet for months. Of course, they were using it for free and got offended at my suggestion of paying for access, which was critical for my business. So, we decided to part ways. Most other complaints followed the same pattern.

One user kept persisting, sending us complaints for days from throwaway anonymized email addresses which just rejected all replies. About a week later he contacted us from a genuine address, asking that we fix his access or give him a refund. Unlike the insurance company which wouldn't pay for something that was critical for their business, this person was actually a customer but admittedly a touch more paranoid than most people. He lived in a country where the government regularly spied on residents, and he wanted to hide his tracks on the Internet. There was no reason why we'd block that. This was a genuine long-tail behaviour that I'd never considered. In theory, there could be more people like him, but we'd never know because they masked their Internet access point.

If someone wasn't trying to abuse the free tier, they should be welcome to access our product in any way they wanted. We could allow access for VPN users, but only if they upgraded to a commercial plan. Instead of an error message explaining why VPN traffic was blocked, the product started to prompt free users to upgrade. We ended February with a 25% jump in revenue compared with January. Some of those people who

were getting something for nothing decided that it was worth paying after all. (You won't be surprised to learn that the guy who used a VPN for "spiritual reasons" was conspicuously not among them.) As a side-effect of all the sudden interest on Google, we also got a nice bump in search engine rankings and significantly increased traffic for months to come. The Valentine's day rush was a gift after all.

The key lesson here is not to block spiritual users, but to figure out how people are hacking your product. And I don't mean hacking just in the "shadowy figure in a hoodie typing an endless scroll of green code in a tense montage" sense. While it's definitely important to protect your business from abuse, especially if a whole subcontinent decides to go through the back door at the same time, you can also discover useful lizard behaviour if you watch out for people tweaking your work or combining it with something else for an unintended use case.

In *Product Led Growth*, Wes Bush suggests splitting potential user goals and problems into beginner, intermediate and advanced categories. Users will initially need to be successful with beginner tasks to establish basic trust and confidence in your product, but they'll then graduate to more complex use cases. This is a nice restatement of Bruce Tognazzini's Complexity Paradox.

Product Led Growth suggests developing a monetization strategy around that graduation threshold. Offer beginner tasks for free, but then request that people pay for intermediate and advanced usage. Making audio files while hiding your tracks on the Internet definitely isn't a beginner-style problem. Discovering long-tail users who needed to do that helped us uncover another reason why people might want to pay for access.

Track support patterns

You can also discover unexpected use cases by reviewing support questions and complaints. During the *Customer Success at Scale* fireside chat in 2019, Rachael Neumann spoke about how customer support is often a source of untapped opportunity for product development. Neumann is the founding partner at Flying Fox Ventures and former managing director for Eventbrite in Australia. According to her, organizations tend to view customer service as a cost centre instead of a strategic centre, so customer service is usually the first function that's off-shored or cut to save money. Neumann warned that customer service personnel "are basically speaking to hundreds or thousands of customers a day creating rich data sets that are never captured, mined or used".

Benefitting from customer service information might require an organizational change, mandated from the top. In the January 2012 *CEO of the Internet* article for *Wired* magazine, Steven Levy interviewed Jeff Bezos about Amazon's vision for perfect customer experience. Bezos said that it's "one in which our customer doesn't want to talk to us", explaining that every time a customer contacts Amazon, they "see it as a defect". Product managers aim to understand why that contact happened and try to prevent such interactions from occurring in the future. Just to make this clear, Amazon isn't actively trying to stop people contacting the service agents, but instead trying to make the product so good that such interactions aren't necessary. A quote that stuck with me from that interview is: "People should talk to their friends, not their merchants." (Note to Jeff: this is why Alexa failed.)

Out of sheer necessity when working on MindMup, we adopted a view that every support email was basically a symptom of a UX issue. There are just two of us

doing everything from pre-sales to development and customer support, and we'd never be able to grow the service if it caused a lot of support issues. As much as possible, we changed the product to allow users to resolve issues themselves. This allowed us to keep support costs low, scale the service without having to hire additional people, and generally spend our time doing more productive work. But it also helped create a very intuitive product that users are happy to recommend. Yes, people should talk to their friends instead of us, but when they're doing that, they might as well spread the word about our product.

Changing the product to reduce the need for support isn't just for small teams. In the *Finding Bugs before Writing Code* presentation from the Atlassian developer conference AtlasCamp 2016, Sigurdur Birgisson defined the goal for supportability as "we need to help the users help themselves before they ask us for help". This kind of twist on support isn't possible by just

involving customer service personnel, developers or testers. It crosses into product management.

Product management should be deeply involved in customer service, both to feel the pain of bad decisions and to get insights for future development. Connecting the two sectors was easy for MindMup, because those roles were filled by the same people. In larger organizations this is much more difficult, but it can and should be done.

Rachael Neumann, in her fireside chat, suggested creating a role that sits between product management and customer support, responsible for analysing customer support data, providing this as insights to product management, and then coordinating feedback from product updates.

Another option to bridge this gap is to involve product managers in customer support occasionally.

A good product manager needs to be first in line to talk to customers after the launch. That's relatively easy when you only have a few customers, but as products mature, organizations tend to put more layers between delivery teams and customers. This frees up product people to work on new features, but it also breaks the customer feedback loop. If you're a product manager, spend a few days per month directly working with customer support people. Speak to real customers. Get actual feedback.

Involving product managers in customer support might sound impossible to pull off in larger organizations, but it's just a matter of policy. In *Working Backwards*, Colin Bryar and Bill Carr talk about the Customer Connection programme at Amazon, which effectively achieves a similar thing. Every two years, anyone above a certain level in Amazon, including the top managers, has to become a customer service agent for a few days. This helps to keep executives up to date with customer issues and provides valuable insight for ongoing initiatives.

I'm not suggesting that customer support is somehow trivial so it can be done by anyone. People with product management responsibility have a different skill set from customer service agents, so they might need help or training to effectively support customers. That's why the Customer Connection programme at Amazon involves a training refresher. (Presumably, in Amazon's case, including how to handle all the Tolkien fanboys moaning about "factual inaccuracies" in the Rings of Power...)

Instead of fully providing support, product managers could also listen in on conversations or sit next to customer service staff as they reply to emails, instant messages or forum posts. Alternatively, product managers could listen to a sample of recorded conversations or occasionally read through customer support message threads and forums.

If your competitors have a public support forum, this can also be a great source of relevant ideas. If someone else has already paid for a mistake, there's no reason for you to repeat it.

Engage with outliers personally

When you have lots of users, it's easy to fall into the trap of just looking at big trends and patterns. That's definitely useful, but aggregate data cannot convey emotions. Speaking with individual customers can help you spot excitement and frustration. It can also point to outliers that hide in the long tail of statistics. Such examples can be a hugely important source of insight and inspiration.

I still vividly remember a message from a MindMup customer with an impressive number of expletives, insisting that we stop sending approval emails. At that point, MindMup didn't actually have any email-sending functionality or an approval process. I politely replied that the person contacting us must be confused, and that they probably wanted to get in touch with some other provider (and, ideally, an anger management counsellor). "No", the reply came back, with another batch of expletives and a screenshot of their email inbox. The image contained a message with our logo and a thread of several hundred similar emails.

At first look, this seemed as if someone was impersonating us. But on closer inspection, the emails seemed to be from a public cloud storage provider requesting access for our application. Back then, MindMup enabled users to store data through several public cloud providers. This was important because it allowed people to keep their data secure without having to trust

us. At the same time it reduced our operational costs, since someone else was paying for storage. Using a third-party storage provider requires an application developer (us) to register an application with the cloud provider (e.g. Dropbox or Google Drive). The storage provider then allows users to activate the application for their account. During registration, we had to provide a logo for the application, so the cloud provider was using it in the approval emails. That was one mystery solved. But I couldn't figure out why those emails were being sent in the first place.

When a user wanted to save some data in the public cloud, our application needed to ask the cloud provider for authorization on behalf of the user. The first time when we did that for a specific person, the cloud provider software popped up an authorization request in the user's web browser. Once the user signed in and approved our access, our application got a security token and could access the user's public cloud storage.

This was all relatively straightforward and took only a few seconds for most people. But not for the person who contacted us. Somehow he was getting hundreds of emails instead.

The unlucky email recipient was a university IT administrator. The university didn't want students to be able to approve access on their own. Instead, when a student confirmed that they wanted to save a document, the storage provider sent an email to the administrator for final approval. A professor had recommended our tool in a popular online lecture, several hundred students had wanted to try it out, and the administrator's email inbox had become rather overloaded. Ultimately, the emails weren't coming from us but from the cloud provider, and they were caused by a specific configuration at that university.

It seemed there wasn't much we could do, so I suggested to the administrator that the university's

After reading some cryptic documentation from the cloud provider, we found the missing configuration parameter. It took just ticking a single checkbox in the application configuration, and the administrator could then pre-approve access. This configuration tweak increased our usage more than months of developing features (and, crucially, caused a drastic drop in the number of F-bombs landing in my inbox).

The whole process with two-stage approvals seems to have been an afterthought for the cloud storage provider, implemented a bit clunkily and probably added hastily as university administrators complained. Instead of just approving storage requests, the administrator actually pre-installed our application for all student accounts at a university. All of the sudden, even students who didn't explicitly request our app were discovering it in their accounts. And many of them tried it out of curiosity.

Lots of other university and company administrators had similar two-stage configurations, but they probably never experienced such a rush in demand to annoy them enough to contact us. Once we enabled bulk approvals, all these people were pre-installing our applications for all their users, leading to significant growth in our product usage for years.

policies might be too strict. Perhaps the university could think about relaxing the policies for our application, so that students could approve access directly. This time we got a reply without any expletives. The administrator told us he'd be happy to do that, but the option to pre-approve our application was disabled in the cloud provider panel. With similar applications, the administrator claimed he could evaluate the first few requests and then just approve the rest globally using "admin installation". That option wasn't available for our application, so the university got hundreds of manual actions instead.

When working with a large number of users, you'll definitely not have the capacity to talk to everyone. Don't let that be an excuse to completely disconnect from your users. People fitting into global patterns might not require your attention, but when someone does something seemingly crazy or sends a strange email, consider that this might be an opportunity for genuinely new insights. It might be worthwhile for product managers to occasionally engage with such outlier cases personally, while customer service personnel are handling all the regular cases.

Lizard Optimization helps you remove unintentional obstacles

Fixing outlier problems may not seem economically justifiable. Long-tail users represent a statistical rounding error compared with primary user categories, and improving the product to handle outlier cases may not seem worthwhile if it disrupts technical code elegance or adds more complexity to the product.

Instead of thinking about adding unjustified complexity to the product, think about removing unintentional obstacles from it. Users in the statistical long tail are struggling because the product is placing obstacles between them and their goals. Those obstacles can come in many forms. They could be caused by bad user experience, by unintuitive workflows or by missing features. If you focus on removing obstacles, Lizard Optimization becomes less about fixing outlier issues and more about helping users succeed.

Fixing an outlier issue doesn't stop you from losing one customer; it prevents a whole class of people from leaving. This is because of what I'll call the *Law of the Mute Majority*: for every person who angrily contacts customer support, there are likely hundreds who don't say anything. They just give up.

Additionally, believing that fixing outlier issues is economically unjustifiable is limiting thinking to just the effects for current users. Having a lizard pop up on your radar can be a signal of a totally different group trying to use your product, perhaps for some new and unexpected use case. Discovering those new types of users can unlock a lot of growth. People doing seemingly crazy things might turn out to be a statistically important user category if you help them succeed with your product.

Of course, you shouldn't follow each individual lizard blindly. That's the economically unjustifiable part. Trying to please everyone will create a product that's not good for anyone. The key thing is to use the long-tail behaviours as an inspiration to improve the product where it matters most. This is where the second step of Lizard Optimization comes into play...

ZERO IN ON ONE BEHAVIOUR CHANGE

The Narakeet audience started to grow like crazy in early 2023, and web traffic surged so much that the business became financially unsustainable. When the audience was growing relatively slowly, the ratio of free to commercial users was balanced. A small percentage of people, those who upgrade to a commercial plan, are effectively financing the operational costs for themselves and for free users. (And when I say "operational costs", I mean everything up to and including our single-origin coffee expenditure. Thanks!)

As growth accelerated, the free users were joining much faster than commercial users were upgrading. We were getting a huge bump in traffic but we were also running out of cash to pay for that increased attention. (Our coffee budget was under threat!) We had to find a quick way to grow sustainably.

To solve a critical business problem, it's crucial to focus effort on one specific outcome. Otherwise, you risk delaying that key achievement. In *The 4 Disciplines of Execution*, Chris McChesney, Sean Covey and Jim Huling call out the most important difference between organizations that are good at execution and those that just waste time. Their first rule is simply "Focus on the wildly important." It sounds obvious, but why then do so many organizations fail at this? I doubt that anyone in charge of a product ever said "Let's just spend a bunch of time doing unimportant stuff."

The problem is that product work rarely delivers value instantly. While big business outcomes (such as sustainable growth) are great to set the vision for the longer term, they're not the right thing to track in the short term. The second most important practice from the *4 Disciplines* book is not to wait for long-term goals to materialize in order to evaluate work. It's trivially easy to say whether something succeeded or failed a year after you launched it in the market, but by that time it's too late to recover from mistakes. Instead, the trick is to find leading indicators of value: things we can measure relatively quickly and cheaply, but that can tell us we're going in the right direction. If the wildly important goal is a destination on a map, then a leading indicator of value is akin to a GPS tracker pointing to the next turn on the road, or alerting us if we've missed it. (And I guess the investors are akin to bears on the trail: always hungry, dangerous when startled, best appreciated from a distance.)

To get back to growing sustainably, Narakeet had to restore the balance between free and commercial users. Users had to go through a free trial more cheaply. (Of course, more cheaply for us, not for them. The only way we could make an already free trial cheaper for the users would be to pay them for the experience. While that might be a valid growth strategy for companies with venture capital to burn, we did not have that luxury). Another option was to get users to upgrade sooner, or get a larger percentage of free users to buy a commercial plan. Those three changes would be good leading indicators that our work was going in the right direction.

Our first try to make the free trials cheaper was to reduce the available capacity. Free users could create up to 20 audio or video files. Allowing trial users to make only up to 10 media files immediately reduced the costs but didn't solve the problem. In fact, it made it worse. The average user wasn't becoming confident enough with the product to upgrade after just 10 free experiments, so the conversion rate from free to commercial users dropped significantly. Reducing the free task allowance ended up being a costly mistake, but at least it was a valuable lesson. It established that the number of free files was directly correlated with the number of people upgrading to commercial accounts.

The balance between free and paid accounts could also be restored by getting users to upgrade more frequently. If we increased the number of free tasks, perhaps more people would experience the product as valuable and decide to upgrade. Doubling the free allowance to 40 audio files got the percentage of people upgrading back to the old levels, but it didn't significantly improve the numbers beyond that. The users who weren't convinced by 20 free tasks just wanted something for free and ended up using the increased capacity to the maximum without upgrading.

Both experiments had failed, so we restored the allowance back to 20 media files. Because the initial two experiments showed that we shouldn't be changing the number of allowed free tasks, perhaps we could reduce how much each of those tasks was costing us. That way, users could go through the free trial more cheaply.

Our operational costs are directly dependent on the amount of text processed into speech. Commercial users could turn entire books into audio files, but we didn't want to allow that for free users. At the time, the limit for each voiceover script was 5000 characters (that's 5000 letters or numbers, as opposed to an ensemble cast to rival Game of Thrones). Halving the allowance to 2500 characters per audio file caused no significant impact on the rate at which free accounts were upgrading to paid accounts. Finally, some good news. Costs were still too high, but this was a step in the right direction. We halved the free task capacity again, reducing the allowance to 1250 characters. When that also didn't cause a drop in customer upgrades, we halved it again. The final change caused a negative impact, so the actual boundary was somewhere in between. In the end, we set the limit to 1000 characters, and things started looking a lot more positive.

Expect lots of bad ideas

This kind of trial and error is typical when working on products that experience rapid growth. Upfront user research can somewhat reduce bad assumptions, but it can't eliminate them. This is especially important when audience demographics are changing, such as during a period of rapid growth. (Doubly bad news if your assumption was "my audience will never change".) The new audience might not have the same preferences or expectations as previous users. When working on something unfamiliar, we need to expect a lot of errors.

In the *Online Experimentation at Microsoft* report by Ron Kohavi and others, the authors conclude that "only about 1/3 of ideas improve the metrics they were designed to improve". One third of the ideas evaluated in the report didn't move the numbers at all, which means that roughly one third actually damaged the very thing they were supposed to improve. The research covered only experimental ideas, not everything that Microsoft works on. (They did not have the courage to include Clippy). The paper also quotes examples of organizations where all ideas (not just experimental ones) need to be validated, and the success rate was about 50%. Products growing quickly might be significantly more uncertain. Mike Moran has some statistics about Netflix from 2007 in *Do It Wrong Quickly*, claiming that the organization considered "90 percent of what they try to be wrong".

Expect this percentage to get even worse when dealing with lizards. If working on new product ideas is akin to a throw of dice, then focusing on an outlier is like picking a lottery ticket. You can achieve disproportionally successful outcomes, but the odds are also a lot more brutal. In effect, the key quality for a product manager working on Lizard Optimization is knowing how to pick lottery tickets. But this doesn't mean that we're left relying on pure luck. Unlike a fully random lottery draw, there are things you can do to improve the odds in product management. One of the key tricks is to keep the focus on outcomes, not on the work to reach those outcomes...

Focus on the impact, not on the effort

In order to know which ideas worked out and which failed, you need to be able to evaluate the outcome quickly: is it good, bad, or time to grab your go-bag and cross the border?

Reducing the number of free media files for Narakeet from 20 to 10 sounded like a good idea, and it did reduce operational costs as intended, but it didn't achieve sustainable growth. Because we had a clear outcome set upfront, we could recover from a mistake quickly. The target outcome was defined so that it was not dependent on any particular work that could lead to that result. It was a problem statement, not a specific solution. This allowed us to evaluate different options for solutions and ultimately judge whether our actions made sense. (For example, buying cheaper coffee could reduce our operational costs, but it would be one of those things that in this universe do not make sense).

Identifying good leading indicators of value is key to stop ongoing work that will turn out to be a waste of time. It's also critical for discovering the opposite – those ideas that have a surprisingly good return on investment – and pushing them more strongly. To do that, the indicators of value need to describe the problem, not the product features. They also need to be observable relatively quickly after we do the work. Observations need to be objective, ideally measurable by some external factor rather than relying on people's opinions. In addition, such measurements should be relatively cheap and easy, otherwise people will look for indicators of those indicators.

Use behaviour changes as indicators of value

Behaviour changes are amazingly good leading indicators of value. If we do some work that causes our users to do something important faster, more cheaply, better or more easily than before, we're clearly providing value to them. If we invest in improving a product and our users still do the same things in the same way as before, then we just wasted time. If we act on a seemingly good idea, but our users' behaviour changes in the opposite direction of what we expected, then the idea backfired. Those measurements are externally observable and objective, and not just someone's personal opinions.

When reducing the allowance for the Narakeet free tier users, the wildly important goal was to keep growth sustainable. Knowing for certain whether the company can grow without too much risk would have required a few months to see how things played out. By that time, it would have been too late to fix the impact of bad ideas. Instead of waiting to see whether we were on the right path or going bust, we defined potential leading indicators through user behaviour changes. Then we tested different ideas by looking at how our users' behaviour was changing. The first few attempts failed. Then something worked well.

Focusing on behaviour changes allowed us to track whether we were solving the problem, not whether we were delivering the solution. This distinction is subtle, but describes one of the most critical skills to master for good product managers. Without identifying concrete behaviour changes to track, it wouldn't have been possible to influence delivery so rapidly. We could have ended up overconfidently jumping off a cliff or gold-plating solutions and unnecessarily delaying other important work.

Create a scoreboard

The final two disciplines in the *The 4 Disciplines of Execution* are to create a good scoreboard to track change, and to establish a cadence of accountability. McChesney, Covey and Huling suggest that "if you're not keeping score, you're just practicing"; therefore, you're not actually competing.

The scoreboard should track changes in a way that's objective and, ideally, quick and cheap. This is another place where behavioural changes come in quite useful.

The cadence of accountability is influenced by how frequently we can extract reliable measurements for the scoreboard. The nice thing about behavioural changes as indicators of value is that we can measure them in many different ways at many different levels of confidence. For example, for a web-based product, we could measure behavioural changes using analytics from a live product version, tracking actual users, using two groups for a statistically relevant experiment. Alternatively, five test users could try out potential product changes on an experimental version of the product that's only available in the testing environment. These ways of measuring value come with significantly different costs and significantly different levels of confidence. Based on the available time for evaluating changes and the potential risk those changes introduce, we can decide how much to invest in making sure that our work is actually valuable.

From the perspective of Lizard Optimization, once we've identified some weird behaviours, we can start thinking about how those behaviours should change or how the product should change to support those behaviours better. We can then try out some ideas that have a reasonable chance of supporting those outcomes. Finally, we can compare the actual impacts to the expected behaviour change to evaluate whether things are going in the right direction. We can track whether someone's doing something differently from before. We can even measure by how much, to decide whether we need to do additional work.

Monitoring behavioural changes may not provide certainty, but it provides a good indicator of the direction in which things are developing. Until someone invents an Instant Lizard Brain-Reprogramming Baseball Cap, changes will take time to materialize. We might not be able to quickly change everyone's behaviour fully or achieve the magnitude of change that we might have

hoped for, but we should see at least some movement in the right direction with at least some users. That's usually enough to provide focus for delivery. Douglas Hubbard suggests in *How to Measure Anything* that good metrics don't need to eliminate uncertainty, just reduce it to acceptable levels. (After all, not everything is as high stakes as heart surgery, aviation, or making coffee with an upside-down Aeropress.)

Solve a smaller problem, don't deliver a partial solution

One nice aspect of focusing on behaviour changes is that we can deliver value incrementally. This becomes critical for getting fast feedback, which is important to quickly spot mistakes.

If helping all our users do something faster, better or cheaper would take too long, we can solve a sequence of smaller problems. When the outcome is defined as a behaviour change, there are two good ways to create a smaller problem:

1. Help a subset of users, or
2. Cause a smaller behavioural change

Both options allow us to get faster feedback while still achieving something good.

For example, a small percentage of Narakeet users tried to convert text to speech in the wrong script. They'd try to get a German voice to read Russian Cyrillic text, or a Hindi voice to read English text. At the time when I wrote this, most AI voices knew how to read only one specific language. We pay the voice providers based on the number of characters sent in a request, but we charge users based on the duration of the audio produced. This meant that we'd have to pay even when someone tried a crazy combination of scripts and voices that produced no audio output, but our users wouldn't be paying us. To make things even worse, users would complain that the audio was blank, increasing support costs. Some were just becoming frustrated with our product because they got stuck trying to convert text that the chosen voice couldn't read, without ever realizing that they were doing something unsupported.

To fix voice/text mismatches fully, we'd have to build a reliable language detection system. An initial estimate was that a proper solution would take months. But we could start to solve the problem for a subgroup of users immediately. For example, Hindi has a unique script, as do many Indian languages. There's no ambiguity in that use case, and the script is easy to detect. By solving the problem only for a subset of users, those who wrote only in Hindi, things could get moving pretty quickly.

The first iteration of the solution just attempted to get Hindi users to be more successful at converting text to speech. We showed them a good error message if the chosen voice wasn't trained for Hindi, and measured whether they recovered from the problem and ended up creating an audio from the same text. This took less than a day of work. A small percentage of users got back on track, which provided a nice confirmation of the idea. Most of the people were still getting stuck, though, and just randomly selecting other voices.

The second iteration was to guide users towards a solution by listing only the compatible voices in a drop-down menu instead of showing the error message. Still focusing only on Hindi users, and only when they had a single-language script, this solution looked a lot more promising. It took a few days to implement, but the success rates improved so much that further fixes for Hindi weren't needed.

The third iteration was to help users of other languages with unique scripts. People writing text in Chinese, Korean and other Indian languages got a much better experience after just a few more days of work.

Breaking a bigger problem down into a sequence of smaller problems helped us to take smaller steps when working on something highly experimental, and to deliver value sooner. But this still leaves the question of selecting which behaviour changes to focus on in the first place.

Follow the stages of growth

A useful way to choose the right outcomes to work on is to apply the stages of growth model from *Lean Analytics* by Alistair Croll and Benjamin Yoskovitz. In the book, the authors show that successful products tend to evolve through five distinct phases. I find it incredibly helpful to think about what stage of growth my products are in at a particular moment, and to choose the appropriate outcomes aligned with those phases. The five stages of growth are:

1. *Empathy*: figuring out how to solve a real problem
2. *Stickiness*: building the right product to keep users around
3. *Virality*: growing the user base (I'm using the original name here, but for more traditional organizations you may want to rephrase this stage to talk about market share or user-base growth)
4. *Revenue*: establishing a sustainable, scalable business model
5. *Scale*: consolidating the business operations

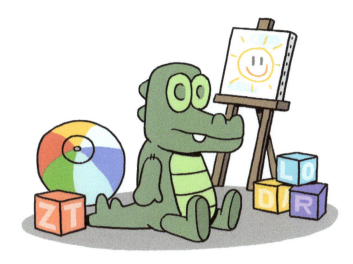

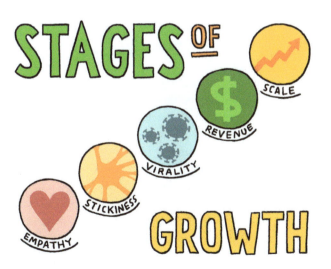

Proving empathy

In the initial stage, we need to prove that we're actually solving a problem for someone important. Some relevant group of users should start doing something differently once they interact with our solutions. Achieving that means there's possibly a product that can evolve around those ideas.

The target behaviour changes for the initial phase should focus on the intended primary use case and make it simpler, easier or faster than users could do without the product. For Narakeet, this was getting people to make videos more easily from slides. For MindMup, this was to help users create and publish simple mind maps quickly.

Unless your product is in the financial market, then focusing on anything related to money would be wrong at this stage. Similarly, unless the product is aimed at social networking, then focusing on sharing and social interactions would be wrong at this stage. Those are all important behaviours, but you can address them later.

Proving stickiness

In the next phase, we need to prove that the solution matches an important problem for the chosen audience (product/market fit). Frequency and urgency of usage are typically good signs that we're on the right track. If early users frequently reach for our product, that's a good indicator that we've solved an important problem in a good way. If not, the solution either doesn't cover enough of the problem to justify repeated use, or the audience is wrong.

The user behaviours in focus for the second phase should be relatively similar to the ones used in the first stage, but with different intended changes. In the first stage, we need to make some important work faster, easier or simpler. In the second stage, we need to get users to do it more frequently or sooner than before. For Narakeet, the key metric at this stage was the number of videos an average user created in the first few weeks of engagement.

It's quite usual in this phase to find a different audience to focus on, or to iterate on the solution until it

becomes good enough for the selected group. This is when the first big pivot happened for Narakeet. We started with the idea of making videos from plain text files, but ended up focusing on making videos from PowerPoint presentations. People were making marketing videos from PowerPoint slides much more frequently than from text scripts, and we iterated on the web interface to assist them.

Proving growth potential

The first two phases usually involve early adopters and help product managers select the right audience. In the third phase, products need to prove that they can actually reach the target market. A good indicator of this reach is that the number of users and customers starts growing rapidly. If the number isn't growing, it's probably best to focus on marketing or features that provide value to larger groups of users. It could also be that the target market is out of reach because incumbent competitors have too much power. In that case, it's common to iterate on an alternative approach or find a segment of the market that's very receptive and focus the product on that. (The more drastic option, "eliminate competitors by any means necessary", is a subject for a future book. Assuming I haven't already been taken out by then.)

The user behaviours in focus for this stage of growth are usually tied to the selected growth engine. For example, for a product intended to grow through organic online search, the focus should be on getting visitors to discover the product more easily and to start engaging with the product more frequently after landing on a web page. For products intended to grow through social network effects, the focus should be on getting existing users to share created content more frequently online, to invite their friends or to reshare content from other users.

Proving revenue viability

Once we've proven that the market is reachable, the next thing to prove is that we can sustainably extract enough value from that market. A good indicator of

that is that the audience we reached is willing to pay for the experience, and pay enough that the product makes a nice profit. This phase usually includes covering wider use cases, offering additional things that could be sold along with the primary product, and generally putting the incoming money under solid control.

This is the phase where revenue optimization becomes critical. Product managers should focus on getting customers to pay more frequently, set up larger subscriptions, or commit to spending larger amounts of money in the future.

Consolidating for scale

In the fifth phase of growth, companies usually focus on improving scalability, systematizing processes and getting operational aspects under control, to sustain working at scale. In the fourth step, we optimize incoming money flows. In the fifth, we optimize outgoing money flows. We can do that by improving the operational aspects of a product, reducing the cost of servicing users, and reducing the cost of deployment, support, manufacturing and similar factors.

Set both targets and constraints

The idea of stages of growth is to focus on optimizing one area at a time, and in the right sequence. There's not much point optimizing operational costs for a product before we can prove that it can grow and bring in revenue. It's wrong to focus on revenue extraction if the market is unreachable or too small. We'd be wasting money on marketing if the audience dropped off immediately after trying our product. There's a logical sequence of these outcomes, and we should choose the wildly important goals according to the product growth stage at a given point in time.

However, this doesn't mean that we completely ignore later phases during early work. A product might need enough revenue to pay for ongoing development and support, and enough scalability at an acceptable cost to allow any growth. The way I use this model is to focus on one area to improve, and use the others as constraints. One area points to the direction on the road; the other areas help create safety barriers that keep us in the right lane.

For example, in the growth phase, we should set targets for the number of active web visitors or active users, or for market share. But we should also define the constraints or acceptable levels for stickiness, revenue and scalability. A trivial way to increase usage is to make the product completely free, but that might damage revenue too much. On the other hand, it might be perfectly acceptable to grow and sacrifice a bit of revenue or increase operational costs. What's too much? What's acceptable? Such tradeoffs are a product decision, and that decision needs to be made explicitly before we start changing stuff.

In early 2023, Narakeet was in the third stage of growth, so in theory the focus should have been on

bringing in a larger audience. However, operational costs were no longer acceptable. Focusing on features that would bring more users to the web site would actually have been damaging. It was critical to get operational costs under control. On the other hand, optimizing operational costs beyond what was needed for growth would also have been wrong. For that specific time, the right thing was to improve revenue or reduce costs just enough to go back to acceptable levels, then support growth by focusing on other things that could help us reach a wider audience.

Setting clear targets and constraints is also important for spotting second-order effects, when our work causes further unexpected changes. When we set

constraints explicitly, we allow people to make quick decisions and spot if a situation is getting out of hand before there's too much damage (cue Michael Caine complaining "You're only supposed to blow the bloody doors off!"). In *Trustworthy Online Controlled Experiments*, Ron Kohavi, Diane Tang and Ya Xu call such constraints "guardrail metrics". I like that name, as it creates a visual metaphor of keeping us on the right path.

You can use the stages of growth to figure out which kind of behaviours would be sensible to improve at a specific moment. Is your product in the stickiness phase? Look for ways of getting users to stay around for longer, to come back more frequently, or to use your product more urgently when they have the problem

you tried to solve. Is the product in the virality/growth stage? Look for ways to get users to share your product more frequently with their friends, to use it with larger groups, or to recommend it more easily or more frequently. Then potentially set some objective targets for changing those behaviours, and guardrails for viable solutions using the other stages of growth.

Clearly identifying important behaviour changes along with targets and constraints helps to focus Lizard Optimization and prevent costly mistakes. Instead of us acting on every crazy idea that comes up in research, this can help us choose the problems that will have the biggest impact. Once we know what problem we need to solve, we can actually try to implement a solution.

REMOVE OBSTACLES TO USER SUCCESS

A common way to focus product development on one particular segment of the market is to create a "user persona", a fictional character representing a specific subgroup of a product's target audience, embodying those people's behaviours, goals and pain points to guide design decisions. Lizard users won't fit into your personas (or personae, for lizards with a bent for Latin). They might have the same goals as the main persona abstractions, but their behaviours and pain points will at first seem strange.

When lizards show up with their problems, many product managers tend to dismiss them or even actively fight against unusual demands for the sake of staying true to the original strategy. Don't confuse product vision and tunnel-vision. What seems to be lizard behaviour could be an indication of a wider set of obstacles. As the user population grows, the new people might be facing different challenges compared with initial users. Identifying and removing those new obstacles is crucial for unlocking faster growth, as it can help a product address a larger market.

Focusing on a single persona is key to launch a successful product. Expanding the reach to a wider audience is often necessary to grow the product.

Detect when a solution becomes an obstruction

Narakeet started as a tool to make simple slide-show videos from images and voiceover scripts. I was frequently making short demonstration and documentation videos for posting to social media. It usually took me several hours to create a simple five-minute video; we're hardly talking *2001: A Space Odyssey* here. I hated how much time it took to record audio, edit it and synchronize it with visuals. A quick poll on LinkedIn identified a few dozen people with very similar needs,

enthusiastic to try something new and provide feedback. These people seemed to be technically savvy, knew how to capture screen recordings and screenshots, and needed to create demonstration or documentation videos. For these people, an ideal solution would allow them to upload images (often screenshots) and short video clips (often screen recordings demonstrating some action) along with a script for the voiceover, and the tool would just magically do the rest. The first version of Narakeet did exactly that. It recorded the voiceover using realistic text-to-speech engines, merged and synchronized audio and visual assets, and generally did all the boring and repetitive tasks – freeing users to get on with something more important (or secretly watch Netflix). It reduced the time to create demonstration videos from hours to minutes.

As the product started getting traction, I expected that the audience would expand beyond the initial persona. Every time anyone got in touch by email with a question or suggestion, I tried to convince them to spend 10 minutes with me on a video call. The pitch was usually something along the lines of "The product is new, so the documentation is a bit incomplete, but I'd be happy to show you how to use the tool in person." From the users' perspective, they'd be getting a personalized demo from the founder. From my perspective, it was a chance to keep tabs on my user population and see their workflows in action.

Some people were uncomfortable manipulating image files, and many didn't have screenshots or recordings ready when trying to create videos. Some users weren't even making demonstration videos; instead, they were creating marketing clips or short announcements.

Many of the people in this category used PowerPoint or something similar to plan their video flow. Even before they could start using Narakeet, they needed to export each slide as an image then struggle to find those files on their local devices in order to upload them. Several users added the key voiceover ideas into presenter notes under their slides while planning the flow, and had to copy those chunks of text later into a single document. This was an error-prone process, as people often mixed up versions of slides and the sequence of text notes.

Making a video from images removed a big obstacle for the primary persona, but was actually an obstruction for new users. The product was adding friction and making it difficult to even get started.

Help users escape the suck zone

In *Badass: Making Users Awesome*, Kathy Sierra suggests reviewing user experience at several key milestones, from first contact, through being able to do the basics, to becoming competent and achieving mastery. The most vulnerable time for users, according to Sierra, is in the "suck zone" – the period between first exposure and when a user can do the basics.

Sierra also suggests figuring out the "bigger compelling context" in which people use the product, and helping them become highly successful ("badass") at that. Instead of making videos, the bigger context of our product was publishing learning materials. We needed to help users become great at that. Nobody wanted to become badass at exporting images and updating chunks of text. (Although I'd be intrigued to see a *Justice League* lineup that includes JPEG Man and his trusty sidekick, Flash Upload.)

In the wider context of publishing learning video materials, our users were getting stuck in the suck zone by having to spend too long preparing content. Aiming to help marketers get out of the suck zone quickly, we added the option to upload PowerPoint presentations instead of individual images. Users no longer had to export slides to images and copy and paste voiceover from presenter notes; the product would automatically do it for them.

The new user persona turned out to represent a much larger population than the initial one. Marketers told their colleagues from enterprise learning departments about a way to turn slides into videos, and they started producing online training courses. Corporate educators spread the word to teachers at universities, who were very enthusiastic about the ability to convert existing lecture slides to video lessons. All these

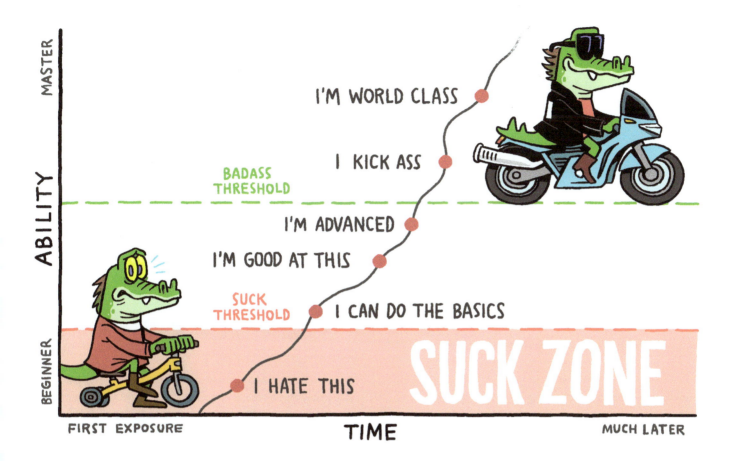

different categories of users had the same goals and the same obstacles as the marketer persona.

During the six months of public beta testing in 2020, our users created more than 100,000 videos. More than 90% were converted from PowerPoint slides. Removing obstacles for the new persona created 10-times product growth. Equally important, the PowerPoint people were creating much longer videos compared with the original group. Demonstration videos were short, usually five minutes or less. Training courses and lectures ran for hours. One person

even uploaded a PowerPoint with 1100 slides, making a 20-hour video. (It was a vocabulary language lesson and not, as I'd first suspected, the latest Peter Jackson epic.) Narakeet billing is proportional to the duration of the videos people create, so people using PowerPoint had a much larger average customer value than the initial persona.

There are two important points in this story. The first is that different categories of users face different types of obstacles. Identifying new personas and new obstacles is key to unlocking growth by addressing different market segments. The second is that we should always be on the lookout for tangential information. Spotting that many users planned their videos using PowerPoint and that some of them used presenter notes to track the voiceover script helped create a totally new user interface that significantly reduced friction. (Power-Point? Reduced friction? It's tempting to make a joke about slides here, but that'd be a slippery slope.)

Let lizards evolve into new personas

Ongoing user research can help uncover new personas and potentially new directions for a product, but it's difficult to scale. Early on I could afford to speak personally to almost anyone with a question, because there weren't that many users. Once thousands of people started engaging with the product, speaking to everyone was no longer viable. Spotting lizard behaviour can provide similar results to user research, especially if you pay attention to information about unexpected usage.

Late in 2020, the largest user groups for Narakeet were marketers, enterprise learning teams and educators. All those people needed decent videos, but they weren't video professionals. The visuals they could produce from PowerPoint were adequate for their needs. Video making was valuable for them, but not the biggest draw of the tool; that was actually text-to-speech conversion. Teachers, marketers and enterprise content creators could record professional quality audio from a script without having to find a sound-proof room, buy professional recording equipment or, above all, cringe at the sound of their own recorded voice.

Text-to-speech engines were already available online, but getting them to work well required a lot of technical knowledge, beyond what those people could achieve on their own. Narakeet made it easy to use the latest AI voices without learning the technicalities. One of the key

innovations was to control audio completely using just the presenter notes in the slides. Users could, for example, just add a note in brackets to increase the speech volume or to change the voiceover language. This was much simpler and easier than the (quite technical) speech-synthesis markup-language standard used by the competition. We called these notes "stage directions".

One user complained about the audio quality when combining several stage directions in the same video slide. I downloaded the project to investigate it, and quickly found what was wrong with the audio. I was, however, surprised that the video was blank: it was just a white background with a voiceover. Either this user was trying to create a low-budget virtual reality simulation of a snow storm (classic lizard behaviour) or the video assembly pipeline had a much bigger issue than audio quality.

My first guess was that something unexpected in this particular PowerPoint broke our image conversion so all the slides came out white. I loaded the presentation in PowerPoint, and my surprise turned into serious puzzlement. All the slides were actually blank.

People used all sorts of weird tools to make presentations; sometimes the third-party apps had bugs when saved in PowerPoint format. I assumed this was one of those cases, but was concerned that we weren't catching the problem. We'd be charging people for producing blank videos, and they might blame us for the broken visuals or ask for refunds.

Our product should at least show a decent error message if it can't load the visuals, so I asked the customer what program he'd used to create the document. It turned out it was the official Microsoft application, which turned my puzzlement into total confusion. I asked the user to load the presentation on his device, which he did, and to check whether the slides showed anything; he said they didn't. I suggested that perhaps the presentation wasn't saved properly or included some unsupported legacy image formats, but the customer replied that the slides were intentionally white. Wait a moment, why would someone be paying us to create blank videos? That made no sense.

Double-checking that the blank video wasn't a mistake, I learned that the user was a professional video editor, and that the visuals he could produce using Power-Point were nowhere close to what his clients needed (admittedly, the simple pleasures of WordArt and slick transitions aren't for everyone). On the other hand, the ability to control the audio with stage directions made Narakeet way better than other text-to-speech tools he'd tried before. Our stage directions removed so many obstacles for that user that it justified creating blank videos with the voiceover just to pull out the

audio track, which he could then use in a professional video-editing tool.

This wasn't someone doing something crazy, it was a completely new category of users getting value in an unexpected way. This lizard evolved into a completely new user persona: someone who doesn't care about video output at all, but who values audio quality and productivity when working with text-to-speech voices.

For this new persona, the PowerPoint approach added a lot of unnecessary friction. The user had to copy the voiceover text into slides, breaking it into chunks to fit the allowed capacity per slide, then upload the presentation, wait for conversion, and finally extract the audio track. Making the audio was actually a tiny part of assembling a video, so users would unnecessarily wait for the audio to be merged with a blank canvas. The user interface was putting unnecessary obstacles in front of this persona.

To help these users, we needed to remove even more obstacles and allow them to directly upload a text file. They could then use stage directions to quickly produce voiceovers without needlessly creating blank slides.

The process became much faster and easier for users who just needed an audio file, but it also had significantly reduced operational costs (as it was skipping the video-assembly process). Initially, I thought that we could pass these savings on to our users and charge less for audio-only conversions. To get the first version out quickly, though, we just charged the same for video and audio files. Nobody really complained about that – and, like most founders, I'm not morally opposed to making money – so the price stayed the same. That means the new persona is significantly more profitable for the business compared with old user groups.

The new tool also removed an important obstacle for other users, because it enabled them to review voiceovers much faster. Marketers and educators often want to tighten up the voiceover script after watching the video for the first time. The audio-creation process is technically just a tiny part of the video conversion, so the text-to-audio tool was much faster at providing an audio sample for feedback than the video- building tools. Instead of waiting several minutes for video conversion to happen before reviewing the voiceover, users could now fix their voiceover scripts in seconds.

The text-to-audio tool took off much better than expected. Initially a very small group of people were using it, but they were amazingly engaged. A month later, there were half as many audio tasks as there were video conversions. A few months later audio conversion overtook video production, and it seemed to bring a completely new group of users in. What was a fringe use case quickly became the main driver. And the number of audio conversions kept growing, bringing in new categories of users, leading to more optimizations and new use cases. At the time when I wrote this, audio conversions accounted for more than 99% of user tasks. Finding one user who created blank videos led to more than 100-times growth. Thanks, snow lizard!

Expand personas using spectrums

Spotting lizard behaviour can help to identify new personas with completely new use cases, but it may also be a sign that an existing persona is wider than expected.

Personas are a useful tool for product management, but they're simplifications and abstractions, and as such they're necessarily incomplete. If our assumptions about users represented by a persona are wrong, then the product might be unintentionally placing

obstacles between users and their goals, forcing them to do weird things to work around those issues.

Because of the Law of the Mute Majority, for every person who manages to get through the UX equivalent of the Minotaur's maze with enough energy to complain through support channels, there are probably hundreds of people who just give up. Detecting and removing unintended obstacles can help retain those users. A nice example of that is a curious bug report we received for MindMup...

MindMup is a collaboration tool, initially designed for larger screens and keyboards. We expected people to use it mostly on laptops, and potentially to review updates on smaller (phone) screens. We didn't account for the fact that, in the late 2010s, stuff that has no business connecting to the Internet all of a sudden started becoming "smart". A cynic might say that the appliance manufacturers started becoming "smart" and realised that they can extort money from users with subscription charges, paid updates and ads. Washing machine makers looked at social networks with envy and decided to copy the worst behaviours. Android screens started to pop up in the most unlikely places. Microwave ovens demanded access to the home Wi-Fi. (And trust me, you don't want to see their search histories...) And so, one day, we got a complaint that our software didn't work well when used from a fridge. What was this user trying to do? Mind map their lunch menu using a salami? I had so many questions that I didn't even know where to start.

The user reporting the issue was a busy mother, trying to collaborate with colleagues at work while cooking lunch for her kids. She had a laptop in another room and a phone nearby, but both were inconvenient to use while she was moving around the kitchen. The smart fridge had a large display and a browser, so she tried to load our software there. This whole thing still sounded a bit nuts (refrigerated, of course), but I could see some logic in it.

Our chilled mind-mapper wasn't trying to do something completely new. Her use case was just a behaviour of a wider persona. An existing user was trying to achieve the same value as before, but admittedly in a weirdly different context. Although we didn't rewrite the software to work with kitchen appliances (my apologies to anybody who's desperate to stimulate critical thinking with an induction cooker), this and a few similar "bug reports" led us to redesign the main toolbar to work better with touch screens and not require a keyboard so much. This made the product more accessible to people who weren't sitting next to a laptop.

Having a clear definition of key personas is critical for focusing delivery, but accepting some fuzziness around that is also very useful to keep users engaged. So how do we keep the focus but also widen the reach beyond narrow simplifications?

Kat Holmes presents a potential solution for expanding the definition of personas in *Mismatch: How Inclusion Shapes Design*. When people struggle to use a product, Holmes interprets it as a mismatch between the design and users' abilities. For example, if the instructions aren't clear enough or the interface isn't intuitive enough, users might not understand the task they need to perform. And no, I don't mean "because my pet lizard has more brain cells than the user", however tempting it may be to jump to that conclusion.

The mismatch depends both on the user's cognitive abilities and the situation. Someone with dyslexia may be unable to read the instructions in time.

Then again, even the smartest people will have trouble focusing next to a developer hacking away on a retro mechanical keyboard. Similar mismatches can happen in many categories. For example, users might understand the task but not see the buttons clearly enough. This could be because of a disability, such as bad eyesight, but it could also be due to working in a very bright environment or on a device that's running low on battery and dims the display to preserve power.

Holmes suggests tracking the changes in user abilities and usage contexts on a scale from permanent to temporary and situational, calling this view "persona spectrums". A persona spectrum helps us to understand users and their challenges in different situations, so we can consider the design choices and tradeoffs that might reduce mismatches.

Designing products for accessibility and engaging groups of people with disabilities is far beyond the topic of this book, but there's one critical guideline that applies both for inclusive design and Lizard Optimization: "Solve for one, extend to many." The big value of removing obstacles from lizards isn't to help just one person, it's to help improve the product for everyone.

Taking an example from the US Census Bureau and various other US government sources, the *Microsoft Inclusive Design* guidebook provides statistics for one such category: people with upper extremity (arm) disabilities. According to the guidebook, 26,000 people in the US have a permanent disability such as an arm amputation. Around 13 million have a temporary disability, for example injured arm. Another 8 million have a situational disability, for example that of

Permanent

Temporary

a new parent holding a baby in one arm. This means that improving the product for 26,000 people actually helps around 21 million potential users (not to mention the positive impact of not dropping all those babies).

Inclusive design mostly deals with problems that prevent people from using a product, but the same thinking also applies to people doing something crazy or difficult to understand (like fridge-gate), which is important for Lizard Optimization. Applying the persona spectrum to lizards helps us start to unpack the seemingly illogical things people might do. Lizard users have trouble understanding our products or interact with them in ways that we have trouble understanding. For some, this may be due to a cognitive mismatch: the user interface is just too complicated for people at that end of the persona spectrum. But a much larger

Situational

population might just be temporarily or situationally lizards. They're not crazy or stupid. Instead, they could be distracted or influenced by an environmental factor. (These can range from "We've run out of coffee in the office" to truly environmental factors like "Sea levels are rising, forests are on fire and, worst of all, we've run out of coffee in the office.")

The mother preparing lunch for her kids was a situational lizard. Feeding the children was more important for her than sitting next to a laptop to collaborate with colleagues. By changing the toolbar, we didn't help only her; this would be economically silly. We helped a whole range of people on the same persona spectrum who didn't have access to a keyboard or who preferred to use a touch-screen display.

With any product that is at least a bit popular, someone will try using it on a beach under direct sunlight, in the dark while someone else is sleeping, or mid-air while dangling from a search and rescue helicopter (don't ask). And if you're really lucky, your product may be so popular that someone will even try to use it on a fridge. These are situational impairments. Making users suffer for that is lazy.

Instead of forcing lizards to run an obstacle course, a product should help them succeed. Those people can help us define new personas or challenge our assumptions about existing users. Good products help people succeed when they're temporarily or situationally distracted, confused or impaired. Great products even help people who temporarily mutate into lizards.

Solve for one, extend to many: improve a product for lizards to make it better for regular people.

DETECT UNINTENDED IMPACTS

Introducing a new product or changing existing features always has the potential to cause unintended impacts. Months of research and careful testing won't protect you from that. If you don't believe me, just ask the designers of the Airbus A380...

The A380 is the largest passenger airplane in the world (or at least it was when I wrote this). It has two decks along the full length and can carry more than 800 people. At an airport, it looks as if a strange beast has descended to feed on smaller airplanes. With four roaring GP7000 engines, it can cover about 15,000 kilometres in a single flight. Emirates airline runs it on a route from Dubai (UAE) to Auckland (New Zealand), taking roughly 16 hours in the air. Each of the engines is about 5 metres long, with 3-metre wide rotating blades, and takes in an air mass flow of about 1200 kg/s. For people who aren't airplane designers, it's a metal can with four massive fans that make a lot of loud whirring noise.

The crew and the passengers need to sleep in the A380 during two full-shift flights. The aircraft designers took great care to dampen the sound to make long journeys more enjoyable. Still, during the initial flights, people complained, but not in the way the designers expected. Emirates airline pilots said the jets are so quiet they can hear "every crying baby, snoring passenger and flushing toilet", according to Dave Demerjian's article *Pilots Complain the A380 is Too Quiet for Sleeping* in *Wired* magazine from December 2008.

Unintended consequences are particularly likely when working on something that we're unfamiliar with or uncertain about. Lizard behaviours are unpredictable by definition. Lizards do strange things, and this includes their reactions to our attempts to help them. Additionally, the whole idea of "solve for one, extend to many" assumes that improving a product for lizards helps regular people. That's a big, bold assumption and sometimes turns out to be wrong. All these factors make it critical to carefully study the systemic effects of our work and look for unexpected impacts.

Assumptions are unavoidable, but bad consequences are not

A nice example of why it's important to monitor for unindented impacts is an attempt to optimize payment forms for Narakeet customers in the European Union. The EU generally imposes more bureaucracy than the rest of the world, and corporate customers from the EU need to have their VAT identifier on payment invoices. Our payment processor somewhat supports this process by allowing customers to enter their VAT numbers, and even validates the tax identifiers to prevent typos. Unfortunately, the validation caused more trouble than benefit.

For international invoices, it's common to prefix the VAT number with the country code. For example a French company with the number 123456789 would write it as FR123456789. But for domestic payments, people often use just the number without the country prefix. Our payment processor is a US company, so its work is influenced by international payment conventions. Many of our users didn't know whether the payment they were making was domestic or foreign, and they tried to enter their VAT number without the country prefix. The processor wasn't happy with that and rejected the payment, showing a cryptic error message.

If a potential customer understood English, had enough focus to process the error message, and was used to international payments, they'd finally add the country code and pay us. If the person was someone with lizard logic or they were distracted, then they tried some truly weird things. Some people retried

Payment method

```
☐ Card          ⟎ Alipay
```

card information

```
1234 1234 1234         VIS ⬜ ⬛ ⬜
MM/YY          CVC          🖼
```

Cardholder name

```
Full name on card
```

☑ I'm purchasing as business

VAT information

```
Business name
GB 123456789
```

Pay

payments a few times with the same information, then contacted us to ask why we were rejecting their card number. (We weren't, but the processor showed a message about "numbers" and people assumed it related to credit card numbers.) A surprising number of our EU customers ended up selecting Russia as the tax country, I assume because our processor didn't validate tax identifiers for Russia, and not as part of some convoluted tax avoidance scheme. Then these customers sent

us emails asking for their invoices to be updated. Lots of people just gave up without paying us.

We have very limited influence over the payment forms, and changing validation directly on the payment processor's web site wasn't possible. We could, however, control which fields were shown to users. Kathy Sierra, in *Badass: Making Users Awesome*, suggests that "choices are cognitively expensive". It seemed like a good idea to reduce the cognitively expensive choices by removing the VAT fields from the payment form. We could let people give us money without entering their VAT details. Once they'd finished the payment and gone back to our web site, we could show them a form that we control with VAT fields. That way we could implement our own validation, pre-populate country codes, and do a lot more to assist our customers.

This seemed like a nice example of "solve for one, extend to many". Removing the fields would ensure that long-tail users don't get confused. Because each additional field creates friction and the potential for someone to give up, the fewer fields the better, and even regular users should start completing payments more successfully.

Once the new payment form was active, lizards were no longer dropping off due to the VAT number validation, so the change achieved the intended impact. However, lots of people were confused by the fact that the VAT fields were missing. Instead of paying online, they were sending emails asking how to enter their VAT details. Conversion rates from the EU dropped significantly, almost immediately after the new form launched. The change improved the product for the long tail, but broke it for the middle of the distribution curve. Overall, it was actually better to add the field back, like the noise of an A380 engine, and make the payment form more complicated.

Trust user behaviour, not your instincts

Our assumptions might turn out to be right or wrong, but either way it's important to check them. And when checking, it's important to measure reality with something objective. This is doubly important if different stakeholders disagree about an idea. I learned this the hard way when introducing a brilliant new feature for MindMup.

One of the most common use cases for mind maps is to track academic research. Lots of MindMup users would type something in a mind map node, do a bit of research online, and then expand the mind map by adding related concepts and connecting them together. Then they would do further research on those ideas and repeat the whole process.

I came up with an interesting suggestion for how to speed up the research workflow. A user could type something into one of our maps then press a key on the keyboard (I thought it was particularly neat to use the question mark key). Our software would look up related concepts using Wikipedia and add them to the map, together with key facts and web links. This would reduce the usual research cycle for students from tens of minutes to one or two seconds. We'd make our users, in Kathy Sierra's terminology, "badass" at research. This should lead to students engaging more with MindMup and recommending it to their friends, and perhaps we could even get a few nice write-ups on educational news sites.

David, my business partner and co-owner of MindMup, was against this idea. His instinct was that it was a gimmick, it would just complicate the software for no real value, and it would add one more potential point of failure that would cause support requests. I was determined to prove him wrong and decided to build it anyway. (I've been called "stubborn", but I tend to disagree.)

To prove my point, I had to present solid data. I deployed the feature along with lots of analytics to track user engagement, and split users into two groups – a test population and a control group – so that I could show beyond doubt that automating research wasn't just a gimmick.

After two weeks of testing, I had enough data to confidently show David that he was completely right. It was a stupid idea that added no real value. I deleted the new functionality feeling quite bitter.

Marty Cagan wrote in *Inspired* that product managers often fall into the trap of believing "they can speak for the target customer". Product managers feel that they know what their users want and how they think, but this can turn into unjustified overconfidence. I trusted my instincts so much that at first I didn't even believe the data from the experiment. I assumed the data was wrong. Perhaps that there was a problem with activity tracking, because there was almost no engagement at all coming from the new feature. In the end, the data was right and my instincts were wrong.

I'm not suggesting that gut feelings will always be wrong, just that we can't trust them blindly. Good product managers are likely to have some reasonable instincts about their audience, at least related to users in the middle of the distribution curve. On the other hand, those instincts occasionally turn out to be spectacularly wrong.In 2016, the BBC (the UK's national broadcaster) stopped its MyBBC initiative to personalize the online video player, after spending £75.2 million, as the project delivered no value. The BBC is financed with public money, so the UK's National Audit Office investigated the initiative, and concluded that one of the key problems was that expected benefits weren't tracked. The MyBBC team originally "set a target of eight million iPlayer sign-ups", according to the

article *At the BBC, Agile Means 'Making it up as we go along'* by Andrew Orlowski, published in *The Register* in 2016, but "it did not show in its monthly reporting how many users had registered". (An ironic lack of evidence from the corporation behind the definitive screen adaptation of Sherlock Holmes…) This kind of wilful ignorance and overconfidence allowed the initiative to go on for several years while business stakeholders were changing goalposts and inventing benefits to justify the budget. To prevent this kind of mass delusion for going on for long, we need to track outcomes objectively.

When working on regular product delivery, it might be enough to just track the impact you actually want to create. When trying to change some lizard behaviour, it's crucial to monitor for both expected and unintended consequences. It's difficult enough to predict even what a regular user would do, but with lizards this is almost impossible. Those people self-selected into a group that doesn't follow your logic.

Look out for additional value

Unintended consequences might not necessarily be bad. Some experiments could turn out better than you expected or provide some unplanned value in addition to the primary target.

In September 2022, one of the biggest causes of support emails for Narakeet was users forgetting their account credentials. (If you're in this category, here's a pro tip for memorable passwords: just use your dog's name, but be sure to name your dog something like s&6!459t@ZnQ.) People can set up a username and password login but also sign in through several public identity providers such as Google or Amazon. Users would sometimes sign in one way then come back a month later, forgetting what they selected; they would then try to log in some other way and get frustrated.

(If you're in this category, just name your dog "Sign in with Google".)

Helping users that got confused about the login method demanded a decent amount of support, which was going to become more problematic with time. A potential change that could reduce the problem was to include the login information in the welcome email. I thought about including something along the lines of "By the way, you selected to log in using Google, so make sure to click 'Sign in with Google' next time."

Researching what other products were doing with their welcome emails, I stumbled upon a set of free templates from a popular email marketing application. An example nicely matched what we wanted to send out, but it also had a big, bold call-to-action button. Our current welcome email didn't have a specific call to action, it just listed some links to help people get started quickly. In order to properly try out the

templates, we needed to make the button do something useful. We connected the button to a function to upgrade from a free to a commercial plan.

In a split A/B test, a control group received the old email, and the test group received the new template. The results for returning users signing in were relatively acceptable. The test group complained less frequently about logging in, but they also upgraded to a commercial plan about 30% faster. This significantly helped with cash flow and allowed the product to grow more rapidly.

Lots of experiments won't drive towards the destination that you expect, but there might be some interesting sights along the way that are worth revisiting. When you're looking out for unintended changes, make sure to monitor for extra value or additional benefits. Even if the original test failed and you decided to revert the changes under test, these unexpected nuggets of knowledge might show you your next experiment.

GETTING STARTED WITH LIZARD OPTIMIZATION

Lizard Optimization works well with modern product delivery methods. In general, teams shouldn't have much trouble adopting the technique. To help you get started quickly, this chapter lists some key things to keep in mind as you try to optimize your product for lizards.

Remember that this technique isn't supposed to replace the other things you do for product management (notwithstanding drowning in bureaucracy or having to action terrible ideas that a non-tech exec got from an aeroplane magazine). It's just an additional tool that can help you extract and exploit some additional insight from user actions, especially those that are usually behind your blind spots (or inspired by aeroplane magazine articles).

Make sure you can see when users get into trouble

Operational awareness is crucial for Lizard Optimization, in particular about user actions and behaviours. You need to know when users do something unexpected, seemingly stupid or inexplicable. If you don't already have that insight into user behaviour, start to visualize it. This is good practice even if you don't end up following the other steps of Lizard Optimization. Knowledge of unexpected user behaviours will help you get ideas to improve the product and provide a good way to test your assumptions, even when doing regular product delivery.

If your product is connected to the Internet, don't rely on users to contact you when they experience issues. Add metrics or analytics to discover errors yourself. Make sure to package enough context with each report to at least have a decent idea of what people were trying to do when they ended up at a dead end. Check whether your engineers have a way to track technical exceptions, and perhaps extend that to monitor the information you care about.

In general, I suggest starting with user workflow errors, but there might be other categories of issues that would be interesting to monitor later. These include commercial abuse or security issues. If a single user is regularly getting large discounts or connecting to your web site from hundreds of different locations at the same time, there might be an important product management lesson hiding there.

If customer servicing and product management aren't closely connected in your organization, it's time to bridge that gap. At least make sure that people who are in direct contact with customers forward anything unusual to product managers for investigation.

For products that aren't online or can't monitor and send information back to you, inspect the customer contact points for these insights. It might be possible to get interesting information about unexpected usage by

engaging with user groups and monitoring social media and community platforms. (Personally, I'd stop short of anything involving a telephoto lens and a ghillie suit, but you decide what's best for you.)

Design reversible experiments

When improving the product for lizards, invest in putting some telemetry around the expected changes. Do that even if you think you have a pretty good hunch how things will turn out. Overconfidence can be a lot more expensive than the cost of adding metrics. Don't commit to any specific solution until you can prove that it causes the expected behaviour changes and doesn't cause any adverse unintended impacts.

It's best to consider changes implemented for Lizard Optimization as reversible experiments. Expect lots of experiments to fail. Working with people who we don't really understand requires invention, so it's important to keep in mind that "failure and invention are inseparable twins", as Jeff Bezos wrote in the 2015 letter to Amazon shareholders. Bezos added: "to invent you have to experiment, and if you know in advance that it's going to work, it's not an experiment."

If you have the ability to operate multiple versions of your product in parallel, it's safest to run a split A/B test with a small but statistically relevant trial group. Such a test should show whether the changes you made actually bring value. Otherwise, you might be blinded by global trends. If you can't compare a trial cohort against a control group, then use past information as a baseline. Run the changed version for a while and compare the results with previous statistics.

Set specific improvement targets

When designing experiments, make sure to identify a clear direction for expected user behaviour changes. It's not enough to just set out to improve purchases. Choose whether you want people to purchase larger packages, to purchase more frequently, or to purchase sooner. These three changes all relate to improving purchases, but your product probably needs to be tweaked in completely different ways to achieve each individual impact. All three changes are potentially valuable, but one will be more important than the others at any given point.

If you have enough information to predict the magnitude of change, this will be even more helpful. Aiming to encourage users to make purchases more frequently is nice, but is 1% more frequently good enough? Is 1000% more frequently even realistic? If you decide to define a target, avoid setting a single number. Instead, set a range. Decide on the minimum valuable change. Is it enough to register just one additional purchase? Or do you need users to make thousands of purchases to justify changing the product? Then decide on the realistic target. Anything between those two numbers is valuable enough to keep.

If you can't set a clear target, then just set the direction and try the first experiment. Once you get the results, you'll have more clarity and confidence about how much you can change things in the future.

Don't waste time gold-plating dashboards

To run frequent experiments, you'll need to collect lots of metrics and visualize them in some way. Test results sometimes come from process logs, sometimes from the billing database, sometimes from web analytics, and sometimes from external tools. Automating data collection becomes crucial for efficiently running such experiments, but people sometimes get carried away and try to make perfect dashboards.

Unless you're working on launching an experimentation platform for a multinational giant, dashboards aren't going to be your product. Don't waste time gold-plating them. Instead, spend that time improving your actual product.

Different experiments call for different metrics, and data from individual tests is important only for a short time. Key factors will change frequently, depending on what you test, so you'll be adding and deleting widgets or data to your dashboards frequently. When creating test result visualizations, it's more important to have quick and reliable data than for it to be lit up like a headline act at Coachella.

The exception to this is tracking key behaviours and guardrail metrics that you can use to detect unintended impacts. Those metrics will likely stay relevant and consistent over a longer period, so it's worth investing more in nice dashboards for them.

Ensure you run tests for long enough

One of the most important aspects of setting up a good feedback loop is to get feedback at the right time. Measuring the outcome too early can mislead, because the sample is unrepresentative. Measuring the outcome too late might delay the delivery of value unnecessarily and slow down the next set of experiments.

The mathematical models required for understanding test sample sizes and statistical relevance have been around for a long time; lots of other books and Internet resources cover them, so I won't even try to explain them here. I do, however, urge you to check your data against these models when you're running experiments, in particular to see whether it's time to draw a conclusion or whether you need to collect more data.

When I was starting out with product experimentation, I tried to relearn the probability and statistics courses I'd completed at university. Unfortunately, enough of my brain cells had died out in the interim to make this task challenging, and no amount of coffee helped (and believe me, I tried enough). My good friend Dejan Dimić, a former engineering manager for the experimentation platform at a global food delivery service, saved me from certain doom by recommending a free online calculator for test results. I want to repeat the favour by passing the recommendation on to you... If you don't want to learn the maths but just check your test results, head over to the companion web site for this book, lizardoptimization.org, and you'll find a list of free online A/B test calculators. They can give a reasonable indication of how long you'll need to run a test, based on current data, to notice a relevant impact. They'll also tell you whether the changes you measured are statistically relevant or not.

Start with a road sign; evolve it into bumpers and an alternative route

Many ideas in Lizard Optimization originate with users stuck in some error condition because they did something unpredictable. If you're starting from that position and have an option to deliver iteratively and deploy frequently, a good solution usually evolves through three phases:

1. *Road sign*: Replace a generic failure message with a specific error message. If users currently get an unactionable message, such as "Unexpected error occurred" (which may as well say "To find the answer you seek, first look within"), then isolate the specific cases you want to improve and provide a sensible contextual error message. (Ideally one that doesn't sound like a Zen proverb.) This won't help change things much, but it will give at least some users enough information to resolve the problem on their own. Crucially, it'll also give you a good metric collection point for future improvements.

2. *Bumpers*: Lead users to a solution with contextual actions. Power users might be fine with a sensible error message, but don't expect most people to be able to take appropriate corrective action. Guide people back to safety with clear contextual actions. Display the actions next to the error message so that people can select the appropriate next step and proceed.

3. *Alternative route*: If bumpers don't solve the problem, then change the product to prevent users from ending up in a problematic situation in the first place. (Users keep driving into the sea? Maybe we build a bridge, or a Mario Kart-style jump ramp.) Contextual actions provide a safety-net for people who end up with a problem, and they allow you to try out different solutions without too much risk. You can then try to resolve the issue earlier in the workflow by providing appropriate feedback to avoid the issues altogether.

Try to help lizards all the way

If you had clear targets for the magnitude of behaviour change, don't despair if your first idea doesn't take you all the way. Gerald Weinberg, in *The Secrets of Consulting*, gave us the famous process optimization rule: "Once you eliminate your number one problem, number two gets a promotion." People you try to help might just hit another stumbling block.

Expect to evolve the full solution through several steps, using feedback from previous attempts to come up with better ideas. It's amazing if you get it right first time, but it's more likely that solutions evolve by you learning and improving with each iteration. (Unless, of course, you're in charge of the Star Wars franchise.) This is why it's important to avoid committing early on and to run reversible experiments. You can speed up feedback by solving a sequence of smaller problems, narrowing the target group, or aiming for a smaller change in behaviour.

Each experiment, whether successful or not, is a valuable source of information. If an experiment fails, use the resulting test data to understand why it didn't achieve the desired impact fully. Was it a problem with the implementation, the user's understanding, or something else entirely?

Repeat important experiments periodically

Don't look at an experiment as a one-time task. Humans aren't chemical elements that behave according to a mathematical formula (however compelling this idea might be for the programmers among us). A product's audience can change over time, and it's worth repeating some of the key experiments every few months.

Something that worked marvellously six months ago might not yield the same results today. For example, after a period of rapid growth, the user group attracted to your product may be significantly different from the one you started with. Something that resonated with your early adopters might not have the same impact on new users. Their true needs, pain points and preferences could make your past insights less effective or even obsolete.

Similarly, when new competitors enter a market or existing ones introduce an innovation, the audience's expectations and preferences can change. Unique features that were once exciting can become expected and boring, driving different types of user engagement. People can get used to different user interface interactions based on other products, and new categories of lizards can start to emerge.

By revisiting crucial experiments, we can confirm the relevance of our previous ideas or we can, equally likely, uncover fresh insights that can drive further innovation. If the repeated-experiment results are significantly different from the initial findings, you've just found some new unexpected user behaviours or market trends, offering a fresh opportunity for more optimization.

Keep an experimentation journal

I strongly suggest keeping a log of your experiments and results. There's only so much you can keep in your head, and writing up notes on your hypothesis, expected change and outcomes can help to keep you honest. (Unless your handwriting is tactically illegible, of course.) My journal saved me more than a few times when I was overly enthusiastic about an idea.

The journal doesn't need to be formal, but it should have enough information to help you remember why you decided to implement a specific feature or why you decided to throw something away. Written records can be useful if you need to revisit some functionality or change part of the system in the future.

An experimentation journal is also useful as a collective memory for a team that grows. New people can review old experiments to gain insight into user behaviours and mindsets and understand the reasoning behind past decisions. Knowing that something has already been tried can help avoid making the same mistakes over and over.

Things move very quickly in product development, and a log turns your journey from a wild ride into a tangible data-driven narrative. When you do something inspired by an outlier that unlocks explosive growth, a journal helps to remind you that it wasn't dumb luck but a systematic process of discovery. (Which, in turn, helps you justify a more expensive coffee machine.)

Where next?

The ideas in this chapter are just a quick starting point, but there is a lot more to learn about running product experiments reliably. Once you cover the basics, check out Ron Kohavi's book *Trustworthy Online Controlled Experiments* for a much deeper dive into this topic.

For additional tools and guides and links to all the other books and articles mentioned in this book, check out the companion web site for this book, lizardoptimization.org

SO, IS THIS ALL JUST ABOUT DUMB LUCK?

A big part of the success of Lizard Optimization depends on factors outside our control. Seemingly crazy people need to do inexplicable things; we need to be in the right place at the right time to spot that, and we need a stroke of luck with the product ideas driven by those insights. This process is probably not going to be easy to swallow for stakeholders that want predictable results. Yet, lucky accidents are an undeniable component of modern product management.

Robert Friedel, in *Serendipity is no Accident*, talks about the role of luck in modern science and technology. He points out that given the scale and scope of systematic research, the fact that so much invention is driven by unpredictable and uncontrollable events (such as accidental discovery) is an disconcerting puzzle. A good example is penicillin, which Alexander Fleming discovered in "a series of chance events of almost unbelievable improbability", according to Gwyn Macfarlane's biography. Friedel concludes that "in an activity that is supposed to be fundamentally rational and orderly, this is neither easy nor comfortable".

This doesn't mean that we can rely just on dumb luck. Friedel shows that there's something systematic in how to deal with lucky insights, breaking them down into three different categories named after famous discoverers:

Christopher Columbus set out to find a western sea route from Europe to India, but found a route to the Americas instead. "Columbian serendipity" happens when you look for something, find something else by accident, and recognise its true value. (Not to be confused with Colombian Serendipity, which is I presume an after-effect of illicit substances.)

The Greek polymath Archimedes of Syracuse was thinking about how to calculate the volume of a golden crown without damaging it. While taking a bath, he had the famous Eureka moment. (This is not me encouraging you to join your next online meeting from the tub, but if you turn the camera off, will anyone really know?) "Archimedean serendipity" is when you do something by accident but gain insights into the knowledge that you were actually searching for.

Galileo Galilei, the Italian astronomer, engineer and most recently famous for being a Bohemian Rhapsody verse, heard about a refracting spyglass built by Hans Lipperhey. He designed an improved version, pointed it at the stars, and started a revolution in astronomy. "Galilean serendipity" is when you set out to do something intentionally, achieve it, but also find additional unexpected value.

In all three cases, "insight is every bit as important as the accident", argues Friedel. Pure chance is not enough for discovery. Accidents happen to everyone. To truly benefit from serendipity we need to recognise something valuable when it occurs.

If the whole process sounds too much like trial and error, remember that this is also a perfectly acceptable scientific technique. In fact, it's the core of the scientific method. And, of course, experimentation is not the same as throwing random stuff at a wall to see what sticks. There is a lot more to deliberate experimentation than making a bunch of mistakes quickly. We need to learn from those mistakes.

In the BBC documentary *Fermat's Last Theorem*, the Japanese mathematician Goro Shimura gave a wonderful quote which stuck with me. Fermat's conjecture is a mathematical problem that was torturing scientists for 350 years until it was proven by an accidental discovery by Shimura's colleague Yutaka Taniyama. (Unfortunately, Taniyama died before the documentary was filmed, so couldn't be interviewed.) Shimura talked about Taniyama's process: "Taniyama was not a very careful person as a mathematician. He made a lot of mistakes, but he made mistakes in a good direction so eventually he got the right answers. I tried to imitate him, but I found out that it is very difficult to make good mistakes."

Lizard Optimization helps us make the most of our luck. The first two steps of Lizard Optimization help us build operational awareness so that we can invent on purpose. The second two steps help us make good mistakes.

Now, go and finish trimming your Bearded Dragon.

BIBLIOGRAPHY

Books

Alexander Fleming: The Man and the Myth, by Gwyn Macfarlane, published by The Hogarth Press in 1984, ISBN 978-0674014909

Badass: Making Users Awesome, by Kathy Sierra, published by O'Reilly Media in 2015, ISBN 978-1491919019

Do It Wrong Quickly: How the Web Changes the Old Marketing Rules, by Mike Moran, published by IBM press in 2007, ISBN 978-0132255967

Founders at Work: Stories of Startups' Early Days, by Jessica Livingston, published by Apress in 2008, ISBN 978-1430210788

How to measure anything: Finding the Value of Intangibles in Business by Douglas Hubbard, 3rd edition published by John Wiley & Sons, ISBN 978-1118539279

Inspired: How to Create Tech Products Customers Love, by Marty Cagan, 2nd edition published by John Wiley & Sons in 2017, ISBN 978-1119387503

Lean Analytics, by Alistair Croll and Benjamin Yoskovitz, published by O'Reilly Media in 2013, ISBN 978-1449335670

Mismatch: How Inclusion Shapes Design, by Kat Holmes, published by The MIT Press in 2020, ISBN 978-0262539487

Product-Led Growth: How to Build a Product That Sells Itself, by Wes Bush, ISBN 978-1798434529

The 4 Disciplines of Execution: Achieving Your Wildly Important Goals, by Sean Covey, Jim Huling and Chris McChesney, 2nd edition published by Simon & Schuster in 2022, ISBN 978-1982156985

The Design of Everyday Things, by Donald A. Norman, revised edition published by Basic Books in 2013, ISBN 978-0465050659

The Failure of Risk Management: Why It's Broken and How to Fix It, by Douglas W. Hubbard, 2nd edition published by John Wiley & Sons in 2020, ISBN 978-1119522034

The Secrets of Consulting: A Guide to Giving and Getting Advice Successfull, by Gerald M. Weinberg, published by Dorset House Publishing in 1985, ISBN 978-0932633019

Trustworthy Online Controlled Experiments, by Ron Kohavi, Diane Tang and Ya Xu, published by Cambridge University Press in 2020, ISBN 978-1108724265

Working Backwards, by Bill Carr and Colin Bryar, published by Pan MacMillan in 2023, ISBN 978-1529033847

Online articles and videos

Amazon 2015 letter to shareholders: Jeff Bezos, https://www.sec.gov/Archives/edgar/data/1018724/000119312516530910/d168744dex991.htm

At the BBC, Agile means 'making it up as we go along: Andrew Orlowski, The Register, May 2016, https://www.theregister.co.uk/2016/05/10/nao_bbc_projects_agile/

Complexity Paradox by Bruce Tognazzini: https://www.asktog.com/columns/011complexity.html

Fermat's Last Theorem, Andrew Wiles, BBC, 1995 http://www.bbc.co.uk/programmes/b0074rxx

Finding bugs before writing code, Sigurdur Birgisson, Atlascamp 2016 https://youtu.be/b99UBDkZPkQ?si=7qf4Z_aYPzk9tvbz&t=469

First Rule of Usability: Jakob Nielsen, https://www.nngroup.com/articles/first-rule-of-usability-dont-listen-to-users/

In conversation with Jeff Bezos: CEO of the internet: Steven Levy, Wired, January 2022 https://www.wired.co.uk/article/ceo-of-the-internet

Microsoft Inclusive Design Guidebook: https://inclusive.microsoft.design/tools-and-activities/Inclusive101Guidebook.pdf

MindMup Maps Your Brain in the Browser by Shep McAllister, Lifehacker June 2013, https://lifehacker.com/mindmup-maps-your-brain-in-the-browser-614853279

Online Experimentation at Microsoft, by Ron Kohavi, Thomas Crook, Roger Longbotham, Brian Frasca, Randy Henne, Juan Lavista Ferres, Tamir Melamed, Juan M. Lavista Ferres, July 2009, https://www.microsoft.com/en-us/research/publication/online-experimentation-at-microsoft/

Pilots Complain the A380 Is Too Quiet for Sleeping, Dave Demerian, Wired, December 2008 https://www.wired.com/2008/12/a380-is-so-quie/

Product Led Growth Bedrock Framework: Wes Bush, https://productled.com/blog/product-led-model-bedrock-framework

Serendipity Is No Accident: Robert Friedel, The Kenyon Review, New Series, Vol. 23, No. 2, Cultures of Creativity, pp. 36-47 https://www.sheffield.ac.uk/media/25892/download

Serendipity by design, Milovan Jovicic, https://uxdesign.cc/serendipity-by-design-75fd71d635b6

The Value of Keeping the Right Customers, by Amy Gallo, October 2014 issue of the Harward Business Review https://hbr.org/2014/10/the-value-of-keeping-the-right-customers

The Role of Customer Success Teams in Collaboration with Product Managers, chat with Rachael Neumann, https://vimeo.com/337949688

You can find online links to all these resources at
www.lizardoptimization.org

THANKS

This book would not be possible without the contributions and ideas from many people.

Aino Corry, Aleksandar Simović, Ben Williams, Christian Hassa, Daniel Terhorst-North, Danilo Poccia, David Evans, Dejan Dimić, Jeff Patton, Kent McDonald, Kevin Albrecht, Marcus Hammarberg, Mark Schwartz, Mary Poppendieck, Milovan Jovičić, Per Lundholm, Sigurdur Birgisson and Slobodan Stojanović helped immensely with ideas, discussions and forcing me to keep the content focused and honest.

Mary White copy-edited the content to make it easier to read. Nikola Korać made the whole experience of using this book a more enjoyable with illustrations and visual look and feel. Alex MJ Smith, Adam Hunt, Sarah Rose and Aoife Breen contributed additional content to make this book a lot more pleasurable to read.

Thank you all, and I hope you like the final result as much as I do!